Sustaining Hope

Sustaining Hope

Friendships and Intellectual Impairment

David B. McEwan
AND Jim Good

◆PICKWICK *Publications* · Eugene, Oregon

SUSTAINING HOPE
Friendships and Intellectual Impairment

Copyright © 2021 David B. McEwan and Jim Good. All rights reserved. Except for brief quotations in critical publications or reviews, no part of this book may be reproduced in any manner without prior written permission from the publisher. Write: Permissions, Wipf and Stock Publishers, 199 W. 8th Ave., Suite 3, Eugene, OR 97401.

Pickwick Publications
An Imprint of Wipf and Stock Publishers
199 W. 8th Ave., Suite 3
Eugene, OR 97401

www.wipfandstock.com

PAPERBACK ISBN: 978-1-5326-6721-3
HARDCOVER ISBN: 978-1-5326-6722-0
EBOOK ISBN: 978-1-5326-6723-7

Cataloguing-in-Publication data:

Names: McEwan, David B., author. | Good, Jim, author.

Title: Sustaining hope : friendships and intellectual impairment / by David B. McEwan and Jim Good.

Description: Eugene, OR : Pickwick Publications, 2021 | Includes bibliographical references.

Identifiers: ISBN 978-1-5326-6721-3 (paperback) | ISBN 978-1-5326-6722-0 (hardcover) | ISBN 978-1-5326-6723-7 (ebook)

Subjects: LCSH: Intellectual disability—Religious aspects—Christianity. | People with mental disabilities—Care—Moral and ethical aspects. | Medical ethics—Religious aspects—Christianity. | Church work with people with mental disabilities.

Classification: BT732.4 .M34 2021 (print) | BT732.4 .M34 (ebook)

Manufactured in the U.S.A.   05/14/21

To the sons and daughters,
To their mums, dads, and carers,
To their brothers and sisters,
And to their friends . . .
We see you

Contents

Acknowledgments | ix
Introduction | xiii

1 The Biblical and Historical Background to the Current Situation | 1
2 The Rhetoric and the Reality | 23
3 What Does It Mean to Be Human? | 48
4 The Image of God: Broken and Being Healed | 66
5 The Family and Friendships | 81
6 Friends for Life | 103
7 Living in the Hope | 130

Bibliography | 145

Acknowledgments

THIS BOOK'S ORIGIN GOES back to the many conversations that Jim and David shared over the years that Jim was a student at NTC. One of the key things that we talked about was how the church could journey with those living with an intellectual impairment and their families. Jim has been involved in Special Education for nearly two decades and has read and studied extensively in the field of intellectual impairment and theology. He and his wife also have their own personal experience as parents of children living with intellectual impairment. David is a lecturer in theological and pastoral studies, with a special focus on the theology of John Wesley and its practical application in everyday life. He has been a pastor in the Church of the Nazarene for over forty-five years and encountered many families who have a child living with moderate to severe intellectual impairment. Jim began formally interviewing families and their children who live with an intellectual impairment in 2018 and we are grateful that they talked so candidly about their experiences and shared what they believed were their greatest needs. Their stories and opinions have significantly enriched our understanding in this area and have shaped the content of this book.

I (David) wish to express my thanks and gratitude to several people who were instrumental in helping me in my research and writing. To my co-author Jim, whose own studies at NTC first gave me an opportunity to research extensively in disability studies and how that might be addressed from a Wesleyan theological perspective. Our subsequent friendship and ongoing conversations have shaped this book. I owe a continuing debt of gratitude to my colleagues at Nazarene Theological College, Brisbane. Dr Rob Fringer (Principal) has offered unstinting support for my research work and my fellow faculty members, Dr Bruce Allder, Revd Richard

Giesken, Dr Dean Smith and Dr Linda Stargel, have shared insightful conversations and reflections over these past few years. Teaching several classes at the college on well-being, social justice and disability studies provided an opportunity not only to trial some of this material, but to be enriched by the conversations with the students. I particularly want to thank one of the student cohorts from Perth (Australia) who are themselves deeply involved in ministry to those living with physical and intellectual impairment—Revd Chris Friend, Kellie Parsons, Chimalizeni Mwenda, Rochelle Van Niekerk, Dale Ross and Diane Ryan. My role as Honorary Associate Professor in the School of Religion at the University of Queensland provided me with office space to work and access to the University's libraries and research databases. Dr Neil Pembroke, Associate Professor in Practical Theology and Director of Teaching and Learning at the University of Queensland gave me the opportunity to present several background papers on human personhood at the School's theological seminars which enabled me to further refine some of the critical points made in the book. For many years I have been able to spend the month of June at Nazarene Theological College (Manchester) teaching and being involved in research supervision. This has given me time to use their library for research and writing, as well as the resources of the Manchester Wesley Research Centre. In 2018 I was invited to read a paper at the One-Day Manchester Theology Conference that has influenced several sections of the book. The faculty and staff were gracious hosts and good conversation partners. I wish to thank Dr Deirdre Brower-Latz, Dr Kent Brower, Dr Geordan Hammond, Dr Svetlana Kobnya, Dr Julie Lunn, Dr Tom Noble, Dr Peter Rae and Dr David Rainey for their help and encouragement. Meals and conversations in the Brower home provided many opportunities to talk with Francine about her work in supporting students on the autism spectrum. Eight years ago, I took on the part-time pastoral oversight of the Logan Community Church of the Nazarene and the support of the church family is so important in my life and ministry.

As the interviews for this book reminded us, the love and friendship of the family is beyond price. I want to thank James and his wife Candice, Shona and her husband Aaron, for continuing to be such an important part of our lives. The arrival of our first grandchild, Lukas, has simply added to the joy. Above all, without the constant love, encouragement, and help of my wife Chris, this project would certainly not have been finished.

David B. McEwan

Nazarene Theological College
Brisbane
Australia
August 2020

In 2002 I (Jim) began working at the *Mater Dei* Special School in Sydney and it was there that I came to experience how to build genuine friendships with people living with an intellectual impairment and that it is good to have fun while learning and growing together. In 2007 my wife Melinda and I moved to Brisbane to study at Nazarene Theological College. Through a thoroughly consistent Wesleyan approach, our framework for understanding God and how that impacts daily life was transformed. We want to thank Bruce and Jacque, Richard and Judy, David and Chris, and their families, for this. It was also during these Brisbane years that I worked at Narbethong State Special School. It was here that I experienced an embodiment of the "go to" philosophy outlined in the book. I was befriended by students and staff who showed me the importance of adjusting *my* attitudes and *my* actions to bring the classroom to the student. Today, I work in another first-class education setting with top quality staff. Moss Vale High School is a school community with an embedded belief in the inherent dignity of the individual and the expectation that every person can grow and develop—essential traits for life and work in this area. To my co-author David McEwan: I continue to believe that your understanding and application of the Wesleyan approach is the best fit for the discussion of our book. Your friendship, knowledge and thoughtfulness have helped me navigate through some difficult questions over this past decade. Thanks Dave.

While I truly value teaching in the field of special education, I have an even greater calling and privilege than that. To my wife Melinda: since getting married we have always worked as a team. Your editing, encouragement, patience, and counsel have been crucial in shaping my contribution to this book. I continue to grow in my love, admiration, and respect for you. Our time in Brisbane provided us with the greatest of all the earthly gifts we have ever received—five little Queenslanders! Jeremiah, Ben, Jesse, Charlotte, and Zac—you are five of the best of all imaginable children. Within our small family community Melinda and I have experienced first-hand what the families we interviewed for this book have described. We know the crucial role that genuine friendships can play in helping individuals and families in their journey. We see in the way our children interact with each other, the value and the affirmation that friendship can bring. Without these relationships and these experiences, my role in this book would never have been fulfilled.

To our extended families, you have loved and given much to all of us and we are thankful for your many years of generosity and sacrifice that will forever be remembered. To Ben, Alisa and your children, Bobby, Bailey, Zoe and Beau—you are a significant part of the reason that Melinda and I had wanted to be involved in writing this book in the first place, and an important reason for us to see this project through. To Alan—you are the original creator of *Butterflies and Moonbeams*. To our friends that we have met in and because of a variety of circumstances—during our teenage years at the Church of the Nazarene and the Anglican Church, through one of the many education settings that we and our children have been involved in, and in other circumstances where practical help and friendship was offered during this past ten years. Melinda and I value you and have needed your presence. I also owe a deep debt of gratitude to Teen Ranch in Australia, Scotland, and Canada, as well as The Oakes in England—it was in these communities where I first discovered that serving God and enduring friendships are inseparable.

Finally, for my own mum and dad. You were my first model of what sacrificial love looks like. I continue to be influenced by your example to this day.

Jim Good

Sydney
Australia
August 2020

Introduction

IN JANUARY OF 2017 three families came together for a barbeque. There were five adults and fourteen children under the age of twelve, along with a pet dog. Sixteen of the nineteen people present that day have typically developing intellects. The remaining three people were children who had been diagnosed as living with intellectual impairment in the mild through to severe range and with secondary impairments as well.[1] The parents were very well known to one another, and describe their relationship as particularly close.

It was a noticeably hot afternoon in what had already been a hot summer. The parents were congregating in the shade down one side of the house where the sausages and steaks were being cooked. Most of the children were at the back of the house enjoying some water-play. A large muddy puddle soon developed, and the dog began running through it. Within a few moments she was jumping over everybody with her muddy paws and it wasn't long before the dog needed to be removed to the other side of the house behind a barricade where she and her muddy paws could be more easily contained.

Max, a beautiful boy who would be described by our culture as living with severe intellectual impairment, had been particularly enjoying the commotion. While the other children played around him, Max had been sitting mostly naked in the muddy puddle, enjoying the sensory experience of the water splashing over him as he smeared his body and face with the cool, thick, dark mud. After the dog was removed from the party, Max

---

1. We have chosen to use the term "living with intellectual impairment" throughout the book because we think it is a more respectful way of referring to people, whether the impairment was evident prior to their birth, at birth or through an acquired brain injury. Some of the sources we reference prefer to use the term "disability" or "handicapped."

evidently decided it was his turn to chase the other children. As he was not quite as mobile as the others, he was finding it difficult to catch anyone. He was determined though and, with a wonderfully huge smile plastered over his face, Max pressed on in his game. After a little while the laughter began to fade, and it was apparent that the other children were tiring of Max's persistent attempts to get his muddy hands on their clean clothes. Noticing their emerging frustration, Max's mother quietly removed him to the opposite side of the house where, only a short while ago, the pet dog had been placed. A short time later the other mother present that day joined her, and together they sat with Max in a sandpit. There were tears rolling down the face of Max's mother as she quietly confided in her friend that while the family love Max more than life itself, and he is the source of so much joy to them, there was a deep sadness within her because it seemed that the best option for all involved was to remove Max to the same side of the house as the dog. Through what had now become a torrent of tears, neither of the two women initially noticed that the much loved eight-year old Max had for a few moments been rolling around the sandpit with a soiled nappy. Quickly the two women lovingly helped Max out of the sandpit, entered the house through a side laundry door, gently washed and cleaned him in the bathroom, dressed him again in a new set of his best party clothes, and then re-entered the festivities. All the while the party had "played on" oblivious to what had unfolded on the other side of the house.

Contrast that experience with that of another family who have a ten-year old boy called Sam, who lives with mild intellectual impairment and autism. Sam loves making friends and telling them the same jokes over and over as well as talking about movies and TV shows, but often he only has the family to talk with. Recently, John came from overseas to visit some of his friends here in Australia, including Sam's parents. When he first met Sam, it was at a beach where many families had gathered to celebrate John's arrival. Sam's parents needed some help to manage all their children safely. Since Sam generally has no interest in being in the water, they really needed help with monitoring him up on the sand otherwise they would not be able to join the other families who were splashing in the surf. Maybe in the first instance John was simply doing the parents a favor by helping them out, but John and Sam bonded very quickly and by their second visit to the beach a few days later, John was seeking out Sam and they were spending all of their time together. After that, as soon as the two of them saw each other, both their faces would light up and off they would go to spend time together as friends. It was not a charitable act or a favor to the parents, the two of them wanted to be with each other. John described the relationship as "a real joy for me" and Sam regularly asks, "when can we go and see John in Scotland?" Since returning to his homeland, John has maintained the friendship with Sam and the family through postcards, texts, emails, and phone calls. John's ongoing relationship with them affirms that both Sam and his family are equally valued by John.[2]

What is the critical difference between the two situations? Some may argue that it is the severity of Max's intellectual impairment that limits his ability to relate well to others, whereas Sam, living with a mild form, is able to relate much more easily and can more readily form a friendship. It is easy to blame Max himself for his separation that afternoon and this evaluation only serves to further diminish Max's value as a person. The outcome is to plunge Max and his family into an even deeper pit of isolation and loneliness than they are already experiencing. We believe the critical difference in the two situations is not the level of intellectual impairment that the two children live with, but the friendship offered by John. Both Max and Sam are deeply loved by their parents and siblings, but it was John's actions that communicated something that is crucial to people living with impairment and their families. The incident on the beach was not an isolated event. John spent time with Sam over several weeks, often at the expense of being with other friends he knows. Through this friendship, John was demonstrating that Sam was as worthwhile and valuable as his other friends. John's attitude and actions demonstrated to Sam's parents that someone other than an immediate family member was willing to the spend time to develop a friendship with him, even when John had the opportunity to do other things.

Sadly, Max's experience of life has been very different. Max is clearly loved by his parents and siblings, and on that afternoon, like children everywhere, he wanted to enjoy being in the company of the other children and to join in the games. After a time, the other children wanted to do something different and Max was left on his own. There was no other friend from outside of the family to step in and play with Max for the length of time that he had hoped. In order to let the other children play on their own for a while, and to ensure that Max was not left by himself, his mother quietly withdrew him to the other side of the house. For many years leading up to this event, Max's family had found themselves in the position of regularly having to leave social gatherings (or deciding not to attend in the

---

2. Interview 11.

first place) because they sensed that people were increasingly uneasy with Max's behaviour. And so the tears shed that afternoon were not just about this one moment of isolation, but because it was just one more incident on top of a long list of many similar incidents. One more occasion where the parents had sensed that others felt their much-loved son was out of place in a social situation. One more time spent observing their son on the outside of a friendship circle. One more time when Max's parents had to question whether people believed that Max was as equally valuable and worthwhile as other children. People living with intellectual impairment need to know that they are valuable and worthwhile, they need the affirmation that friendship brings, and they are hoping that people will offer this even if it means that the relationship ends up costing them something. Parents and other siblings need this as much as the child living with the intellectual impairment. The cumulative impact of countless incidents of social isolation over the years was so destructive for both Max and his parents.

These two contrasting stories reveal the crucial importance of offering friendship to *both* the person with intellectual impairment *and* their family. While we all have certain basic physical needs, genuine flourishing for the people who are the subject of this book, requires healthy relationships and genuine friendships to be offered to *both* the person living with intellectual impairment *and* their parents/carers by people outside of their immediate family. These dual friendships are rare, and social isolation is often the result. For all the genuine help that various government, charity, and church programs provide, if the person living with intellectual impairment and their families have no real friendships, then it is always of limited value. The fair treatment of others is critically dependent on whether you see them as a person or not, and the language that we use to describe another person (or groups of persons) sets the framework for our treatment of them. For example, in many Western societies, the use of words such as refugee, Muslim, Jew, black, unemployed, homosexual, or disabled, predetermines how large sections of the society will view and then interact with them. These are words that so often identify a group who "are not us" and therefore they can be treated differently to "our" people. In current Western society, moderate to severe intellectual impairment (whether from birth, due to disease or accident) is identified as a major deficit and questions are then raised as to whether the biological human being is truly a person. While there may well be challenges in forming friendships with people who have intellectual impairment, one of the key areas that raises a barrier is the descriptive language we use. This is true across a whole range of social settings, not just for those labelled as impaired, disabled or "special needs." Our use of language is powerful in determining personhood. Much of it is totally subjective—a person is such because we describe them as such. This is so often based on ignorance or prejudice. So white Europeans did not always think that Africans or South Americans or Australian aborigines were human, and then found scientific and theological reasons to support their views. Similar judgements are often passed regarding those living with moderate to severe intellectual impairment.

At the center of much of the discussion is the notion of the quality of life. In English, quality can be used evaluatively or descriptively, but in our present debates it is the former that predominates, with the notion that any life can be measured against an agreed common standard.[3] The measurement of "quality" can be positive (health and well-being), or negative (impairment). In practice, we tend to focus on pathology and impairments that are easy to detect and quantify, and then social judgements are made as to how to deal with such human beings.[4] A negative evaluation is currently applied by some to those with moderate to severe intellectual impairment. It assumes that people in this situation have very limited life satisfaction and focuses our attention on the impairment rather than the social, political, and economic policies that frame the evaluation. It operates with the assumption that "normal" is a clearly defined and universally agreed standard, and that functioning within this normal range of abilities is in every way preferable and more desirable than unusual, or impaired forms of functioning. This often results in the healthy majority using the concept of normal to express their prejudices, assumptions and fears about the lives and experiences of those they label as "the disabled." It raises the question as to how you score different values and then put them into some sort of hierarchical order, such as physical well-being over emotional well-being, or intellectual capacity over relational engagement? It can lead to decisions that some lives are not worth living, and should not be permitted to continue, because they are considered to have no net positive value or significance as determined by an influential sector of the society.[5] Imagine how a person with Down syndrome (or any other genetically inherited condition), and their immediate family, must feel

---

3. Wyatt, "Quality of Life," 1.
4. Hamel, *Religious Beliefs and Healthcare Decisions*, 7.
5. Hamel, *Religious Beliefs and Healthcare Decisions*, 2.

when government agencies around the world seek to eliminate the conditions by genetic testing and termination.[6]

All this is to say that any evaluation of "quality" or "normal" is never objective, it is always influenced by the assumptions, prejudices and life experiences of the person or group making the judgement.[7] It gives privileged status to one particular perspective, in which the value of one individual life can be directly weighed and compared with others. A form of ethical calculus is performed in which the positive value of one life can outweigh the negative value of another.[8] Some of this is comparatively trivial (for example, some are better than others at singing or understanding quantum physics), but in many cases harshly negative value judgements are made of certain forms of impairment by those who do not experience that particular limitation. No one seriously believes that those lacking the ability to sing well should be excluded from society, but that judgement is regularly made regarding those living with moderate to severe forms of intellectual impairment. If personhood is defined largely in cognitive terms, then the absence or loss of rationality will equate to the loss of self. This is a viewpoint that is commonly expressed in Western contexts. One of the challenges we want to raise in this book is to rethink the framework and the language we use for each other in the context of defining both the concepts of "quality" and "normal." This is where the Christian doctrine of original sin makes a major contribution to the discussion, because it reminds us that every single human being (except for Jesus Christ) is born impaired in some way.[9] None of us are presently as our Creator intended nor as we shall be post-resurrection.[10]

The way that we live together in community not only influences our own personal dignity, but the welfare of the whole group. The flourishing of

---

6. In Western countries, Down syndrome has traditionally accounted for the greatest number of genetically inherited intellectual impairments at birth. Due to the "success" of prenatal testing and termination, that is no longer the case. In Western countries, Fragile X now accounts for the greatest number of instances where a genetically inherited intellectual impairment is present at birth. See CDC, "Fragile X Syndrome."

7. Wyatt, "Quality of Life," 3.

8. Wyatt, "Quality of Life," 3.

9. This doctrine is increasingly questioned in many sectors of Protestantism, but often what has been rejected is a caricature of the doctrine, rather than the theological truth it is seeking to portray. This will be discussed more fully in chapter 4.

10. The nature of resurrection for those living with severe intellectual or physical impairment is currently debated within Protestant evangelical circles. This will be dealt with more fully in chapter 7.

a society is intimately related to the flourishing of the persons in the society and vice versa; you cannot have a healthy society if the people in it are disconnected from each other. Human beings tend to survive and thrive better in groups than in isolation, and it requires not merely a general connection with those around you at the moment, but a range of intimate and supportive relationships throughout life.[11] It has been pointed out that the critical element in so many poor health and well-being outcomes is not simply the lack of social connection, but the quality of the connections. Sadly, many do not want a social connection with a person who has a moderate to severe impairment. Other people have a social connection, but it lacks depth, while others enjoy a genuine friendship. Everyone wants and needs deep, genuine, all-of-life relationships, not just social snippets. This is equally true for people living with moderate to severe intellectual impairment and for their families. Unfortunately, much recent research does not engage the quality of the relationships they study.[12] All human beings have a pervasive drive to form and maintain at least a minimum quantity of lasting, positive, and significant interpersonal relationships. Satisfying this drive involves two criteria: the need for frequent, affectively pleasant interactions with a few other people, and these interactions must take place in the context of a temporally stable and enduring framework of affective concern for each other's welfare—in other words, forming meaningful friendships.[13] It is this lack of meaningful friendships for those living with moderate to severe intellectual impairment and, in many instances, for their families, that makes their lives so much more challenging. This is clearly illustrated by the conversation that took place following the incident with Max mentioned at the beginning of this chapter. Later that evening, during a quieter moment, Max's dad heard of the day's events on the other side of the house. With just the adults present he gently posed the questions that would ultimately provide the impetus for writing this book: "Where is the hope for Max? Where is the hope for us as a family?"

At one stage we had planned to examine a broad range of impairments, but finally decided to focus on those living with moderate to severe intellectual impairment and their families. This is an area that is particularly problematic in Western cultures that emphasize the importance of reason,

---

11. McEwan, "Personal and Community Well-Being," 132–53. See also Butts and Rich, "Acknowledging Dependence," 407.

12. Holt-Lunstad et al., "Advancing Social Connection," 518.

13. Baumeister and Leary, "Need to Belong," 497.

logic, personal autonomy, and independence. It seems to us that our culture particularly devalues those who are living with moderate to severe intellectual impairment, and in many quarters promotes the termination of those diagnosed prenatally, and supports euthanasia for those who experience the loss of rationality in old age. The book begins by exploring the biblical and historical background to impairments and then examines the current situation faced by many families and persons living with moderate to severe intellectual impairment in Australia. We believe that much of the material is equally applicable to other Western nations. Chapter 2 reports on a series of interviews with people around the Sydney area who have a son or daughter living with intellectual impairment, most of whom would be labelled in the moderate to severe range. In some situations, a secondary diagnosis of autism, or physical impairment, or epilepsy was also present. The aim was simple: to ask these families to talk about their experiences and to hear from them what, if anything, they believed people in their local church community could do to support their family. These extensive interviews were recorded and then transcribed before being analyzed. The outcomes identified then lead to an examination in chapter 3 of some of the ways that personhood is defined biologically, philosophically, and theologically, as well as what that means for the establishment of meaningful relationships with others. The importance of every person being created in the "image of God" is then examined from the theological perspective of John Wesley, the eighteenth-century leader and key theologian of Methodism, who upheld the centrality of love and relationships in defining the essential nature of the image. In chapter 4 there is an examination of the damage that was done to the image in the beginning because of failing to live in accordance with God's creation intentions. We then note how God responded in love to bring about healing and restoration through the life, death, and resurrection of Jesus Christ, and how this impacts our relationships with God and neighbor. The key findings in chapters 3 and 4 are: the centrality of relationships in God's intention, God's affirmation of the intrinsic dignity and worth of each individual, and the need to build strong, healthy friendships with all persons. Chapter 5 then offers a range of practical ways to form loving and supportive friendships with families who have loved ones living with an intellectual impairment. In many ways chapter 6 is the heart of this book—how to initiate and build strong friendships with those living with an intellectual impairment. The aim throughout is to promote and enable meaningful friendships with the person and their family, enfolding them within the life of the wider community. We do not want to reduce the person living with an intellectual impairment to a medical or educational problem, or even a ministry program for a local church. The final chapter examines the issue of hope that was raised by Max's father at the beginning of this Introduction. In the light of the resurrection of Jesus Christ, chapter 7 identifies the hope that exists for our present life and the future hope that lies beyond our death. The closing section shows the importance of living now in the certainty of that hope, by affirming the value of every "Max" and building rich friendships with them and their families.

1

The Biblical and Historical Background to the Current Situation

PEOPLE LIVING WITH IMPAIRMENT have been stigmatized throughout history. The human rights movement of the twentieth century and the legislation which arose from it, are important for people living with impairment and their families. This is partly because they have provided an opportunity to redress centuries of discrimination. Most Greco-Roman philosophers suggested that human value is "primarily social value and is determined by potentiality."[1] If a person is not able to contribute to society in meaningful ways, they are considered to have no intrinsic value and are without worth. The Greek philosopher Plato said: "The offspring of the inferior, and any of those of the other sort who are born defective, they will properly dispose of in secret so that no one will know what has become of them."[2] A similar viewpoint was held by his student, Aristotle: "Let there be a law that no deformed child shall be reared."[3] The situation in Roman culture was no different. If those living with impairment survived childhood, they were usually mocked and derided. For example, Cicero wrote: "In deformity and bodily disfigurement there is good material for making jokes" and many vase paintings depicted party scenes where "hunchbacks, cripples, and dwarfs perform for the entertainment of onlookers."[4] It was said that the Emperor Augustus had a granddaughter who "retained a dwarf named Cinopas as a pet," while Plutarch reports on the existence of a "monster market" in

---

1. Amundsen, "Medicine and the Birth of Defective Children," 52.
2. Kelly, "Deformity and Disability," 36.
3. Amundsen, "Medicine and the Birth of Defective Children," 57.
4. Kelly, "Deformity and Disability," 39–40.

Rome.[5] Blindness—the most commonly spoken of disability in both Ancient Greece and Rome—was "regularly (although not exclusively) viewed as a punishment."[6] The prevailing Greco-Roman attitude leading up to and including the time of Jesus was one of "fundamental ambivalence toward the deformed and disabled."[7] Soranus of Ephesus reports that a baby worth rearing is one who is "perfect in all its moving parts, members and senses, with every body part properly moving and appropriately sized."[8] This, sadly, is a viewpoint that remains true in some places to this day.

The Biblical Framework

The situation in ancient Israel and in the centuries leading up to the time of Christ was often not much better. The problem was not so much the Hebrew scripture itself but the way it was often interpreted. Saul M. Olyan argues that people living with physical and sensory impairment (such as being lame or blind) were devalued by casting them as "defective," "cursed" and "profaning of holiness."[9] Such "defective" people (with some exceptions amongst the priestly class[10]) were to be kept from entering the Temple area while they remained unclean—a lifelong fate for those with a permanent disability. In some cases, they were associated with "curses" such as sterility, disease, blight, drought, military defeat, lack of burial, loss of wealth and land. In other cases, they were linked with ideas such as contempt and divine rejection, weakness and ineffectuality.[11] At times in Israel's history, any form of

---

5. Kelly, "Deformity and Disability," 40.
6. Kelly, "Deformity and Disability," 43.
7. Kelly, "Deformity and Disability," 45.
8. Kelly, "Deformity and Disability," 37.
9. Olyan, *Disability in the Hebrew Bible*, 121.
10. A "defective" priest could continue in the temple but was prevented from offering sacrifices to God and could not become the high priest. The priest or potential high priest of Lev 21 who has a "defect" was stigmatized in the sense that his potential to profane the sanctuary's holiness is greater than that of his fellow priests who lack "defects"; in essence, the "defective" priest becomes an ever-present threat of polluting and profaning the sanctuary. Consequently he is a priest who is marginalized within his priestly community because he is cut off from the most highly esteemed ritual activity normally open to him and he is deemed unworthy of several of the central, most honourable privileges. See Olyan, *Disability in the Hebrew Bible*, 31.
11. Olyan, *Disability in the Hebrew Bible*, 103, 121.

impairment could be seen as a result of God's judgement.[12] The Qumran text even associates blindness with the "Spirit of Wrong" and equates it with a reviling tongue, abominable acts, wickedness, falsehood and pride. "Thus, blindness is brought into association not only with a substantial selection of negative qualities, but with the antithesis of the deity himself (the 'Spirit of Wrong' and 'the ways of darkness')."[13] The Temple Scroll also excluded any blind or lame person; they "shall not enter into the city of the sanctuary all their days . . . they shall not pollute the city."[14]

With these stigmatizing attitudes found in Greco/Roman and early Hebrew perspectives on people living with impairments, it should come as no real surprise that we meet many marginalized people in the stories of the New Testament. In the ministry of Jesus there are regular encounters with people living with impairment who have their needs ignored and who are forced to live in anonymity on the margins of society.[15] The devaluation and exclusion of the two blind men of Matthew 20 is indicated by their having to sit on the outskirts of town "by the roadside" begging.[16] The crippled woman of Luke 13 is relegated by religious leaders to a position of less value than a healthy animal. We see Jesus censuring these leaders for their willingness to tend to the needs of their own animals on the Sabbath while questioning his healing of her.[17] The deeply ingrained devaluation and poor self-worth of the woman who has been bleeding for twelve years (Luke 8:40–48) is shown by her daring to only approach Jesus secretively, unsettled at the thought of having public attention drawn to her. The man thought by many to be not in his right mind (Mark 5:2–15) was forced to live amongst the tombs and often restrained by chains.

---

12. See, for example, Deut 28:27–29. This association is quite common in many other passages of the Old Testament.

13. Olyan, *Disability in the Hebrew Bible*, 103.

14. Olyan, *Disability in the Hebrew Bible*, 104. See also Olyan, "Exegetical Dimensions of Restrictions," 38–50.

15. For further reading on the topic of the Hebrew scripture and disability, see Olyan, "Anyone Blind or Lame," 218–27; "Exegetical Dimensions of Restrictions," 38–50; McReady and Reinhartz, *Common Judaism*; Eiesland and Saliers, *Human Disability and the Service of God*; Albrecht et al, *Handbook of Disability Studies*. Olyan argues that the view of "defective" sacrificial animals was likely to have become attached to people who are said to have a "defect." See Olyan, *Disability in the Hebrew Bible*, 30.

16. Hagner, *Matthew 14–28*, 584–88.

17. Keck, *Luke—John*, 272–74.

The Ministry of Jesus

Brendan Byrne describes how Jesus "draws [our] attention to . . . a correct vision of God and of what God wants for human beings."[18] One of the pivotal points in Byrne's argument comes from the words of Jesus in Luke 4:18–19 at the very beginning of his public ministry: "The Spirit of the Lord is on me, because he has anointed me to proclaim good news to the poor. He has sent me to proclaim freedom for the prisoners and recovery of sight for the blind, to set the oppressed free, to proclaim the year of the Lord's favor."[19] This is a quotation from Isaiah 61:1–2, and Jesus applies the words to his own ministry. While Jesus quotes in full Isaiah's phrase about proclaiming "a year of acceptance" he omits altogether "the threatening final proclamation of a day of vengeance of our God."[20] Byrne argues that Jesus was inaugurating a "space" of salvation history (beginning with his life and concluding only when the day of judgement does eventually come at some future, unidentified point) where people are simply accepted and not judged by the Lord. It is a wonderfully generous invitation for "all to come and be drawn into the hospitality of God."[21] This is the point that is often made in the gospel accounts of the life and ministry of Jesus.

Stephen H. Phelps reminds us that there were several actions that were forbidden to a pious man in Jewish society of that era: you don't touch someone who is unclean, you don't touch a woman not of your own family in public, and you don't work on the Sabbath.[22] In sharp contrast to that perspective, Jesus embraced people living with impairments *before* he healed them and *while* they were still considered to be ritually unclean (before they had accomplished a ritual purity that would have allowed for their inclusion). In the story of the woman who was crippled (Luke 13:10–17) we see Jesus touching an "unclean" woman not of his family *and* in a very public place (at the front of the synagogue before the synagogue ruler) *and* on the Sabbath.[23] His attitude towards those who were marginalized in his society was not limited to his actions, he clearly taught how God viewed those who were often disregarded by the religious teachers and leaders of

---

18. Byrne, *Hospitality of God*, 161. For further reading in this very important area, see also Crabbe, "Sinner and a Pharisee."

19. All Bible quotations are from the NIV.

20. Byrne, *Hospitality of God*, 47.

21. Byrne, *Hospitality of God*, 50.

22. Phelps, "Luke 13:10–17," 66.

23. Phelps, "Luke 13:10–17," 66.

his day. In the parable of the "Good Samaritan" told in Luke 10:25–37, a priest and a Temple assistant walked past the badly beaten stranger even though they clearly "saw" him with their eyes. It was another stranger, who culturally would not normally go to the aid of such a person, who not only saw him physically but also paid attention to him and acted generously to help him. In Luke 7:36–50 we have an account of Jesus being invited to a meal at a home where the host (an important religious leader) did not offer Jesus the normal courtesies expected but an "immoral woman" did. In the conversation about this, Jesus asked the man if he had "seen" the woman? He very clearly had physically seen her but had rejected her because of her lifestyle. The leader's attention was held by her immoral life and he did not see her as a person, but Jesus did and because of his attention, her life was transformed. Undoubtedly, Jesus took the initiative to embrace people with impairments. In Luke 13:10–17 we read that when Jesus saw a crippled woman in the synagogue he called her forward, spoke to her, put his hands on her and declared her to be a daughter of Abraham: "Once he has seen her, Jesus takes the entire initiative in this woman's restoration."[24] Restoring the relationship was far more important than the way the religious authorities understood what was acceptable to God.

Walter Brueggemann claims that the word "as" is the best way to explain the different reality used by Jesus to interact with people living with impairments. Jesus saw people "as" someone other than the way they were designated by the surrounding culture. He rejected the false "as" that excluded them and embraced a new "as" that saw them as God's people; he then interacted in ways that were in accord with this true vision. The woman we meet in Luke 13 has been crippled for eighteen years; her society saw her "as" crippled, dysfunctional, and worthless. This was the reality that she had to live with "as" her life. "Jesus counters that 'as' out of the old text of Genesis, renames her, and imagines her otherwise. . . . Jesus enacts a magisterial 'as' that, before the witnesses' very eyes, functions as an 'is.' He refuses to accept the givens of his context and voices a different reality." Jesus saw her "as" a daughter of Abraham, because that is who she truly "is."[25] The long accepted and habituated understanding, rejected by Jesus, is that people living with impairments were ritually unclean, lacked worth and value, and were best kept separate from the community because they might pollute the temple or other people. Jesus asserts a new "as." Importantly, this new

24. Nolland, *Luke 1–9:20*, 725.
25. Brueggemann, *Texts Under Negotiation*, 13–15.

reality does *not* involve treating these people "as if" they are valuable and worthwhile. The problem with "as if" is that it suggests that someone is being treated in a way that is contrary to the truth—someone is being treated "as if" they are valuable when everyone really knows they are not. Jesus treats each one living with an impairment "as" worthwhile and valuable because he knows that they are. This is also illustrated by Jesus' response to the woman who had been bleeding for twelve years whom he had healed physically (Luke 8:43–48). His actions in inviting her to come forward and make a public declaration of what has happened to her are a calculated measure designed to signal that he is not content to leave her cured according to medical definitions only: "He embraces her in the family of God by referring to her as 'daughter,' thus extending kinship to her and restoring her to the larger community. . . . Now she is not the only one who knows what God has done for her; now so too do the crowds gathered around Jesus. Because he has pronounced her whole they are to receive her as one restored to her community."[26] It is important to note that this healing takes place within the framework of a request from a synagogue leader for Jesus to come and heal his daughter (Luke 8:41–42, 49–56). Here is a situation where one might reasonably expect that a synagogue ruler will be favored over a ritually unclean woman. Surely Jesus would seek to prioritize the influential and powerful synagogue ruler; after all, it would appear to be in the interests of his mission to make this significant Jewish man's request a priority. Instead, Jesus takes the time to engage the crowd in a conversation designed to restore this woman so that she will no longer be the object of social ostracism. Culturally, you would not expect that a "social discard" would hold Jesus' attention over and above a synagogue ruler. It underscores that in the eyes of Jesus all people are of equal importance. Jesus clearly considered everyone he met "as" a person created in the image of God, and there can be no prioritizing of some as being more in that image than others. Jesus insists that there is space in God's world for people living with impairments not only to exist but also to flourish. He actively defends and encourages their right to participate fully in the community of faith and in society. This can be multiplied time and time again in his ministry as he fully engages people who live with a range of physical and mental impairments. It is important to note that it is not just the act of "seeing" that is so crucial; it is also the actions that follow the act of seeing. Jesus not only "sees," he then acts to bring about relational reconnection.

26. Green, "Gospel of Luke," 349.

It is this perspective that lies behind Jesus' use of parables to teach God's truth. In Luke 15:1–32 we have three stories about a lost sheep, a lost coin, and a lost son. These parables reveal a person who risks the ninety-nine well cared for sheep to find the one that is lost and vulnerable; a person who searches diligently for one lost coin even while they retain nine times that number in their possession; and a person who risks the good opinion of one son while enduring the social indignity of continually waiting and watching for the return of another son. These parables very clearly reveal that for God, *each one matters*. As Kent Brower reminds us, this is a God who is forever seeking, forever searching, forever waiting and forever longing to lavish hospitality upon those he has created.[27] To God, all people matter equally and all are invited to enjoy his embrace and his provision. Both by his words and actions Jesus insists that there is room in God's world for people living with impairments to exist and to flourish as people of equality and worth. He clearly supports those frameworks that enable people living with an impairment to flourish in their relationships with God and with others. Throughout the gospel accounts we see Jesus interacting with people who live with impairments in ways that perfectly represent God's creation intention to bless and embrace all people. This understanding of God is illustrated in other ways as the New Testament unfolds. We see Paul's concern that he will be marginalized by the Galatians because of his eye problem (Gal 4:13–15). When he first met the Galatian church, he expressed concern that his disabling condition would cause them to reject his message on the basis that his condition could be viewed as a result of sin or an association with evil spirits.[28] It is this common cultural evaluation that caused Paul to write: "Though my condition put you to the test, you did not scorn or despise me" (Gal 4:14). Like many others around him who lived with a physical, intellectual, or sensory impairment, Paul knew personally the stigmatizing and marginalizing effects of disability within both the Jewish and Greco-Roman culture, while celebrating the acceptance he found in Jesus Christ. As Wayne Morris has rightly observed:

> The "perfect" body without a mark or blemish simply does not exist, for bodies—real bodies—are not like that, not even the resurrected body of Christ. So, if we are talking of the church as the body of Christ, and we look to Christ's resurrected body, we are not talking about a body that conforms to an image of perfection according to

27. Brower, "Parables of Jesus."
28. Albl, "For Whenever I Am Weak," 145–58.

social norms and values, but a church that subverts ideas of normality and openly bears the marks it has to show its difference.[29]

In the book of Ephesians Paul reminds the members of the church just how different they are from one another in so many ways and yet he invites them to lovingly submit to one another out of reverence for Christ. In their differences they are to love and serve each other because of their new life together in Christ. Sadly, the church has not always lived up to this truth.

The Historical Background

A negative evaluation of those living with impairment was to persist in Western culture for centuries, despite the teaching and example of Jesus, and the ministry of the Church. Churches continued to offer charitable support and institutional care, though explanations for impairment had not really changed from the classical views of the Graeco-Roman times until quite recently. It is with the rise of modern science in the Enlightenment period that we see an engagement with biological factors as a cause of impairment, though it did not greatly change attitudes to those with the impairments.[30] As Andrew Solomon demonstrates, attitudes in the nineteenth and twentieth century had not greatly improved. Economic arguments were being made about the financial burdens imposed on society by the cognitively impaired and the rise of eugenics provided a medical basis for disparaging them. It was not uncommon to institutionalize such infants soon after birth because of parental shame at bearing such a child (who was usually regarded as not being a real person), and many supported the call to end their lives.[31] Attitudes typical of the times were encapsulated by Samuel G. Howe who commented in 1848: "this class of persons is always a burden on the public. Persons of this class are idle and often mischievous, and are dead weights upon the material prosperity of the state. They are even worse than useless. Every such person is like a Upas tree, that poisons the whole moral atmosphere about him."[32] By the early twentieth century Western medical text books were delineating "how to classify someone an

---

29. Morris, "Church as Sign and Alternative," 56.

30. A full exploration of this topic is beyond the scope of this book. For more information, see Stiker, *History of Disability*; Daston and Park, *Wonders and the Order of Nature*; Wheatley, *Stumbling Blocks Before the Blind*.

31. Solomon, *Far from the Tree*, esp. 179–81.

32. Solomon, *Far from the Tree*, 179.

'idiot,' an 'imbecile,' or a 'moron,' and laws favouring sterility were being instituted."[33] In 1927 Oliver Wendell Holmes wrote, "It is better for all the world if instead of waiting to execute degenerate offspring for crime, or to let them starve for their imbecility, society can prevent those who are manifestly unfit from continuing their kind."[34]

It was not all negative, however. The close of the nineteenth century brought glimpses of a more positive attitude toward people living with impairment, with attempts being made to improve their lives through education and integration. Key to this was the new science of behaviorism and its links with early education which suggested that people are made, not born, and can be educated and shaped into anything. Maria Montessori, who had worked with children in Rome living with intellectual impairment, was one of the earliest proponents of this new philosophy and spearheaded a range of early intervention strategies to improve the lives of those with impairment. Some within other emerging fields, such as psychoanalysis, proposed that the shortcomings of the poor and disabled might be the result of early deprivation rather than organic inadequacy. Meanwhile, the influx of seriously and permanently wounded veterans at the end of both World Wars was beginning to soften social prejudice against those living with impairment in general. Attitudes also began to improve because the eugenics movement ceased to be part of the mainstream after the Holocaust.[35]

The Current Situation

In many Western nations, however, the most significant event for improving the lives of persons living with any form of impairment was the 1948 proclamation by the United Nations of *The Universal Declaration of Human Rights* (*UDHR*). For the first time in the history of humanity there was a single document that articulated the rights and freedoms to which "every human being" is "equally and inalienably" entitled. This is promoted as a document for "every man, woman and child everywhere" and especially for "those who most need their rights protected." The signatories to the document affirmed their commitment to "fundamental human rights, in the dignity and the worth of the human person, in the equal rights of men and women and of nations large and small." In its preamble it recognizes

---

33. Solomon, *Far from the Tree*, 180.
34. Solomon, *Far from the Tree*, 180.
35. Solomon, *Far from the Tree*, 181–91.

the "inherent dignity and the equal and unalienable rights of all members of the human family." In the very first sentence of the first of its thirty articles we read: "All human beings are born free and equal in dignity and rights." Article 2 clarifies: "Everyone is entitled to all the rights and freedoms set forth in this Declaration, without distinction of any kind, such as race, colour, sex, language, religion, political or other opinion, national or social origin, property, birth or other status." Article 7 affirms that all people are "entitled to equal protection against any discrimination in violation of this Declaration and against any incitement to such discrimination." Furthermore, every human being is entitled to the same opportunities in education when and where it is directed to the full development of their personality (Article 26) and to those economic and cultural rights that are indispensable to their dignity (Article 22.) It is not just the isolated individual that is the focus of the document. It affirms that all people have the equal and inalienable right to be part of meaningful relationships, both in terms of marriage and family (Article 16), and our wider social connections (Articles 22, 29, 30). The point is explicitly made that the exercising of one's rights should always be balanced by the need to respect another person's rights and should never be exercised at the expense or the destruction of someone else's rights and/or freedoms. Almost seventy years later the United Nations High Commissioner for Human Rights, Zeid Ra'ad Al Hussein affirmed that "these human rights are not country specific. They are not a reward for good behaviour, or particular to a certain era or social group. . . . They are the rights of people of every colour, from every race or ethnic group, whether or not they have disabilities; citizens or migrants; no matter their sex, their class, their caste, their creed, their age or sexual orientation." The *UDHR* reminds all people everywhere that even when they live in the smallest of places, or even when they have the most significant of impairments, "every human being" is "equally and inalienably" to be acknowledged as having dignity and worth, and be given equal access to their economic, cultural, political, relational and educational rights befitting their status as a human being.[36]

Another of the great "rights" documents of the twentieth century was the *UN Convention on the Rights of the Child* instituted in September 1990. This document specifically stated that "children are not just objects who belong to their parents and for whom decisions are made, or adults in training. Rather, they are human beings and individuals with their own rights."

---

36. UN, *Universal Declaration of Human Rights*.

It applied to all under eighteen years of age and emphasized that individual children are to be valued as contributing members of families, communities, and society. Like the *UDHR* before it, this document once again affirms and recognizes "the inherent dignity and the equal and inalienable rights of all members of the human family." Unlike the *UDHR*, it specifically mentions children living with impairment. Article 23 highlights that children with "any kind" of disability should "receive special care and support so that they can live a full and independent life" in conditions "which ensure dignity, promote self-reliance and facilitate the child's active participation in community." The third of the four points under Article 23 insisted that children with any kind of disability should have "effective access to and receive education, training, health care services, rehabilitation services, preparation for employment and recreation opportunities in a manner conducive to the child achieving the fullest possible social integration and individual development, including his or her cultural development."[37]

Arising from, and influenced by, these documents the right to equality of treatment for people living with an impairment was specifically legislated by many Western governments in this period. For example, in 1990 the *Americans with Disabilities Act* was passed into law in the United States of America. This law prohibited discrimination against individuals with disabilities "in all areas of public life, including jobs, schools, transportation, and all public and private places that are open to the public . . . to make sure that people with disabilities have the same rights as everyone else."[38] In 1992 the *Disability Discrimination Act* was made law by the Federal Government in Australia. This Act made it unlawful to treat a person less favorably, or be given less opportunity because of their impairment or because they are associated with someone with an impairment.[39] Other laws have been instituted that make it illegal to vilify people with disabilities. It is now mandatory that there be equality of opportunity within workplaces for people with impairment. New Zealand decided to legislate that all people were to be considered as equally entitled to human rights without discrimination, and as such there was no need for a specific Act to be passed for people with impairments. The rights of people with impairments were safeguarded in just the same way as they were for any person in New Zealand. The Bill of Rights Act (1990) and the Human Rights Act (1993) enshrined in law that all New

---

37. UN, *Convention on the Rights of the Child*.
38. "What Is the ADA?," para 1.
39. Australian Human Rights Commission, "Disability Discrimination."

Zealanders, including people with impairments, had the right to: the equal enjoyment of civic, political, economic, social and cultural life; education and the ability to access information; the choice of where to live and who to live with; the use of one's own language; to be treated with respect, dignity and equity; and not to be harassed or taunted.[40] In 1995 the Parliament of the United Kingdom passed the *Disability Discrimination Act* to promote equality of opportunity for people with impairments and to make it unlawful to discriminate against them in any way.[41]

The human rights movement and its accompanying disability discrimination legislation, as well as the emerging ascendancy of nurture over nature in early education, have provided a helpful starting point for the reversal of centuries of stigmatization of people living with impairment. These movements have led to many good, practical, and helpful outcomes impacting everyday living for those living with impairment and their families. This is particularly true in Western countries, and includes the work of government, charitable, and church agencies. Many governments require that all public buildings, open spaces, and public transport be accessible to all. In Australia, inclusive recreational opportunities have improved through the creation of a series of all-abilities parks that are fully accessible for children of all ages and abilities. The play equipment is designed to engage the tactile, auditory, visual, and olfactory senses.[42] Government and charitable agencies are engaged in modifying private homes, and even church buildings, to enable easy access and free movement. In the UK the legislation led to "public bodies promoting equality of opportunity for disabled people" and has also enabled an increased push toward supported community housing for people with disabilities as opposed to secluded institutional care.[43] Most western countries seek to provide quality, inclusive education for all who have an impairment. In the USA, for example, there is now a more inclusive philosophy in education with "children with disabilities to be placed where they would be if they did *not* have a disability, to be part of the larger community rather than with a segregated, more homogenous sub-community."[44]

40. HRCNZ, "Disability Rights."
41. Disability Discrimination Act 1995 (c. 50).
42. See, for example, "Accessible and Inclusive Playgrounds."
43. Hedges-Goettl, "Thinking Theologically About Inclusion," 13.
44. Hedges-Goettl, "Thinking Theologically About Inclusion," 13.

Funds are also being made available for family and personal support in a wide range of ways. One of the most comprehensive of these funding schemes was legislated by the Federal government of Australia in 2013 with the establishment of the *National Disability Insurance Scheme*. This is intended to provide for all Australians under the age of 65 who have a permanent and significant disability with the reasonable and necessary supports they need to experience independence, community involvement, education, employment, health, and well-being. It provides people living with impairment, their families and carers with the financial support to access information and referrals to existing support services in the community. The intention is to offer individualized assistance and the flexibility to manage how people receive their support, all focused on helping each person to achieve their goals and enjoy life to the full.[45]

Christian organizations have been formed dedicated to people living with impairment. This includes the *Joni and Friends International Disability Center*, founded in 2007 by Joni Eareckson Tada and John Nugent. This is a ministry committed to "energizing the church to embrace people of all abilities into the fabric of worship, fellowship and outreach . . . [and to] train and mentor people with disabilities to exercise their gifts of leadership and service in their churches and communities."[46] The Christian Reformed Church in America is regarded by some as a model for all religious organizations to follow.[47] In 1993 the Synod of the CRC passed a motion to comply with, and surpass, the requirements of the Americans With Disabilities Act: "The church cannot fulfil its Biblical mandates without making itself architecturally, intellectually and programmatically accessible. . . . To be effective, the church must also find ways in which it can function and have meaning in the lives of people with disabilities."[48] In Australia there are a number of helpful services provided by churches and Christian organizations. For example, *Luke 14* is a CBM initiative "that helps churches become a place of welcome and belonging for people and families living with disability."[49] The initiative encourages people to remember that "our churches will never be complete without an environment that is inclusive

---

45. NDIS, "Understanding the National Disability Insurance Scheme."
46. "Joni & Friends."
47. Pridmore, "Christian Reformed Church as a Model," 97.
48. Pridmore, "Christian Reformed Church as a Model," 98.
49. "Are You Passionate About Social Justice?"

of people with disability."[50] In NSW there is an initiative that began in 2006 called *Jesus Club*. They noticed that "few churches were reaching out to people with intellectual disabilities and teaching them the Bible."[51] The aim of the club is "to make Jesus Christ known to people with intellectual disabilities by teaching the good news about Jesus Christ and forming genuine friendships."[52] It provides churches with the support, training and resources to achieve this aim. The provision of help is not just limited to large cities, and there are significant resources being made available in some country regions to help churches include people with impairment in the church community. For example, Monica Short has researched and written specifically about the inclusive efforts of six Anglican churches in country NSW. They are considered to be exemplars of how to successfully engage, partner and include people living with disabilities within their local area.[53] The congregations are becoming communities "enriched by the presence and ministry of people living with a disability."[54]

The Challenges to Be Faced

These are all good things to celebrate, and life for people with a range of impairments and their families is greatly improved in most cases. Nevertheless, several significant challenges remain in Western cultures that so strongly value rationality, autonomy, and independence. John Swinton writes that the growing use of pre-natal testing within our culture casts a "dark shadow of devaluation" over the lives of people with impairments, even though many would argue that such testing is in no way intended to reflect on their lives "once they are here."[55] Hans Reinders notes that there are two conflicting messages presented by a society that enacts and upholds the human rights/disability legislation, which advocates the equality of all, while at the same time valuing and promoting the importance of pre-natal testing: "The first message says, 'Since you're here, we're going to care for you as best we can,' but the second says, 'But everyone would

---

50. "Are You Passionate About Social Justice?"
51. "About Jesus Club."
52. "About Jesus Club."
53. Short, *People Living with Disabilities*, 12.
54. Short, *People Living with Disabilities*, 12
55. Swinton, *Raging with Compassion*, 191.

be better off if you were not here at all."[56] Melinda Tankard Reist believes that this second message can be identified by the pressure that is placed on couples to terminate the life of their unborn child diagnosed with an impairment. Many of the women interviewed by Reist reported that while a decision to terminate is couched in terms of "choice" there is in fact no option being given to talk to anyone who already has a child living with an impairment. Rather, women are being pressured by worst-case scenarios about particular impairments with the information "often slanted in a way to encourage termination."[57] One woman said: "You get pressured into getting rid of [your child]. They only ever tell you how bad it is going to be. You don't get the choice of talking to someone who's got a disabled child."[58] This societal pressure partly explains the situation in Australia where a vast disparity exists in the termination rates between unborn babies who have a prenatal diagnosis of severe impairment and unborn babies who do not. For example, when Down syndrome is detected prenatally, the termination rate of these pregnancies is now approaching 100 percent.[59] But where no disability is detected, the termination rate of all pregnancies each year in Australia is less than 20 percent. The figures speak for themselves. Reist believes more couples would be likely to choose to continue the pregnancy if they were genuinely allowed to consider and explore that option. This evaluation is supported by her research: "Of the fifty-five couples who contacted the Down Syndrome Adoption Exchange, USA, in 1990 after a prenatal diagnosis, only two decided to place their child for adoption and *none* opted for abortion."[60] Far from being concerned about taking the life of an unborn child who has been diagnosed with an impairment, some doctors are more concerned about missing the detection of a "defective" child. A Melbourne specialist said: "A number of spina bifida cases are being missed in this country and that is a real concern for us."[61] Others argue from an economic perspective and one Australian geneticist has even gone so far as to suggest "if you prevent the birth of a child with Down syndrome

56. Swinton, *Raging with Compassion*, 192.
57. Reist, *Defiant Birth*, 29.
58. Reist, *Defiant Birth*, 30.
59. These figures are not readily available nor easy to obtain, perhaps for obvious reasons. They are extracted from Crispigny and Savulescu, "Pregnant Women with Fetal Abnormalities," 100–103; Romensky, "Down Syndrome"; Mitchelson, "Down Syndrome Abortions"; Right to Life NSW, "Abortion."
60. Reist, *Defiant Birth*, 31.
61. Reist, *Defiant Birth*, 27.

you are probably saving the community a million dollars or more in the life of the child."[62] It comes as no surprise that reflecting on this situation has led one man living with Down syndrome to comment: "[It] doesn't make us feel very welcome, does it?"[63]

The ongoing devaluation of people living with impairment, despite all our rhetoric of the past seventy years around inalienable human rights, can be seen regularly. One mother shared about her experience during a week-long holiday in a resort with her husband and her daughter, who lives with severe physical and intellectual impairment. She noticed how often other families were reluctant to let their children play with her daughter, and often moved away when they arrived. She recounted how so many parents did not deal with their children when they were rude and offensive to her daughter. She says, "I know it can be hard with kids. I get it, really. But imagine if that was your child that you saw ignored and run away from over and over and over again. And it's been happening for twelve years now. You would want to change it for her in some way."[64] In her social media post this mother reveals a range of experiences and emotions that are consistent with our culture's continuing tendency to devalue people living with impairment. This mother values her child and we read of her great love and protective instinct for her daughter, but she senses that others do not value her daughter in the same way, and she simply asks for her daughter to be valued just like any other child. She longs for her daughter to have friends to play with though she recognizes that most of the children she encounters do not share her desire. While parents are no doubt sensitive to how their child living with intellectual impairment is treated, their concerns are not misplaced. This devaluation, even by sympathetic family, friends, and professionals, originates in the implications of such phrases as "handicapped person," "disabled person" or "impaired person." *The deficiency is mentioned first and that cannot help but shape what follows.* While we have started using phrases such as "person with intellectual impairment" to indicate this is first a person, the words themselves have not necessarily led to a change in the old ways of thinking and interacting. Using the more politically correct phrases has not prevented people living with impairment from being seen and objectified in an ongoing way as "the handicapped" or "the disabled" or "the impaired." This tells us that we

---

62. Reist, *Defiant Birth*, 45.
63. Swinton, *Raging with Compassion*, 191.
64. Kyriacou, "How to Talk to My Child."

are still seeing people living with impairment as incomplete persons. This is especially true when compared to the person who is uttering the phrase, who of course thinks of themselves as being whole or complete. For many, these views are not overtly held but are subtly embedded in the psyche. This often leads to dealing with the person and their family as a charitable cause. There is a tendency towards condescension, even when sacrificial support is offered. In most cases the person would be horrified to think of the pain they might be bringing to a family that they love.

This exclusion is also seen in so much of the Western church, which continues to have a poor overall record when it comes to engaging in meaningful ways with people living with an impairment.[65] As recently as 2006 it remained generally accepted that the church "had made little effort to rid itself of the architectural, attitudinal and communications barriers which prevent people with disabilities from participating in the church."[66] This attitude is typified by the fact that some churches in the USA sought an exemption from the *Americans With Disabilities Act*.[67] The church's response is particularly galling given God's intention for it to be a place of hospitality for the marginalized and a counter-cultural community that serves as a foretaste of the life to come.[68] In 2007 it was reported that 71 percent of US congregations said they were "generally aware of the barriers the disabled faced" to participating in church practices. Sadly, 69 percent indicated they "had not yet started or were only getting started at transforming their community 'into a place where children and adults with disabilities are welcomed, fully included, and treated with respect.'"[69] In Australia, less than 5 percent of churches reported having a deliberate ministry of inclusion to people with disabilities.[70] In the UK, Wayne Morris claims that "unhelpful stereotyping of the disabled remained common in British churches and that only 2 percent of British clergy have a disability of any form, even though some estimate that up to 16 percent of the population has a disability."[71]

---

65. Pridmore, "Christian Reformed Church as a Model," 94. See also Hely, "Hospitality as a Sign and Sacrament," 67–80; Hull, "Broken Body in a Broken World," 5–23; Webb-Mitchell, "Confession," 47–55.

66. Pridmore, "Christian Reformed Church as a Model," 94.

67. Pridmore, "Christian Reformed Church as a Model," 94.

68. See Brueggemann, *Prophetic Imagination*; Dawn, *Truly the Community*.

69. Carter, *Including People with Disabilities in Faith Communities*, 7.

70. Gale, "Christian Ministry to People Affected by Disability."

71. Morris, "Church as Sign and Alternative," 48, 53.

Those living with an intellectual impairment face the additional challenge in many Western Protestant congregations because of the tendency to equate a person's faith with their ability to rationally process and annunciate doctrine. The church that primarily seeks to form people spiritually through the intellect will always marginalize people whose intellects are less formed than others. Such people (the list here would include young children, people living with intellectual impairments, and people with dementia) then become relegated to a second-tier class of Christianity or, even worse, regarded as incapable of being a Christian because they cannot cognitively affirm doctrinal content.[72]

From the 1700s onwards, faith and belief increasingly came to be aligned with intellectual assent to propositional truth. Francis Bacon's comment at the beginning of this period was typical of the time: "Resolve to trust your own senses to inform your reasons, and do not superstitiously adhere to the *Ipse dixit* [an assertion without proof] of another."[73] Discoveries in science produced a more certain picture of the workings of the universe as well as the workings of the human mind. Though both of these were still seen as God's creation, it became common to suggest that in some ways God could also be described and engaged with greater certainty using our intellect—God could be grasped in propositional terms by the human mind.[74] Having faith in God became more a matter of the mind than of the heart: "A sure knowledge of God and religious truth was now weighted heavily in favour of what was 'natural' and 'reasonable.'"[75] Consequently religion "must be rational as befitted the mind of God and the nature of man."[76]

> Belief was also becoming a matter of private judgement, for individual reason to adjudicate within the multi-religionism sanctioned by statutory toleration. . . . As religion became subjected to reason, Christianity ceased to be a "given" and became a matter of analysis and choice. . . . As the seventeenth century drew to its close, one call was heard ever louder: religion and reason were one and must pull together.[77]

---

72. For some examples of this, see Swinton, *Raging with Compassion*.
73. Harrison, *Rise of Natural Science*, 101.
74. Rack, *Reasonable Enthusiast*, 30.
75. Rack, *Reasonable Enthusiast*, 30.
76. Porter, *Creation of the Modern World*, 100.
77. Porter, *Creation of the Modern World*, 99.

This understanding of faith as primarily intellectual assent has obvious implications for how people with an intellectual impairment are viewed by Western evangelical Christianity.[78] John Swinton writes:

> In my former role as a nurse working with people who have intellectual disabilities, and then later as a mental-health chaplain, I constantly encountered attitudes and assumptions that seemed to exclude people with profound learning disabilities from having a meaningful relationship with God. . . . A good example can be found in the writings of nurse educator Peter Birchenhall, who observes: "People with profound mental handicap [sic] possess a limited ability to reason at the complex level, and are therefore not able to work through any doubts and develop any sort of faith." In a later article Birchenhall says: "Severely mentally handicapped people are denied the very substance of a rationally productive existence, and are confined to a life of almost total dependence on others for even their most basic needs. Such an existence gives no real opportunity for inner spiritual growth, or the nourishment of the human spirit, both of which are important when coming to terms with the meaning of Christianity. It gives no real opportunity to experience the joy of seeking a lifetime relationship with the Almighty, because the concepts involved are complicated and require a level of awareness which the profoundly mentally handicapped do not have."[79]

A similar conclusion was drawn by Stanley Hauerwas: "The more emphasis that is placed on belief, particularly for individuals, the more the mentally handicapped are marginalised."[80] There are other embedded philosophies within the Western church that tend to devalue a person with an intellectual impairment. James Torrance explains that for the past fifteen hundred years Western theology has been enamored with a concept of the person as a "substance possessing three faculties, reason, will and emotion, with primacy given to reason."[81] Max Turner asserts that a

---

78. For verification and further reading on this point, see Rack, *Reasonable Enthusiast*, 1–39; Harrison, *Rise of Natural Science*, 92–120. For a parallel examination of the emerging trend from the 1900s onwards toward "objectifying" science, see Polanyi, *Personal Knowledge*; *Science, Faith and Society*.

79. Swinton, "Known by God," 141. See also Hauerwas, "Church and the Mentally Handicapped," 59.

80. Hauerwas, "Church and the Mentally Handicapped," 59.

81. Torrance, "Doctrine of the Trinity," 14. See also Grenz, *Social God and the Relational Self*, 171–72.

person's capacity for rational thought and analysis, awareness of self and the possession of an advanced degree of autonomy in decision making are all seen by Western Christianity as prerequisites to the recognition of an individual's personhood.[82] This has resulted in many Christian theologians believing that an individual must possess and demonstrate certain intellectual capacities to be recognized as a person.[83] The word "recognition" is used deliberately here because for some scholars a human being remains a non-person until they satisfy certain conditions.[84] The Christians described here use an individual's development of rational capacities to permit the "recognition" of the personhood they would argue has existed in that individual in a dormant or unfulfilled state all along. However, if "people 'have' personhood rather than 'being' persons," as John D. Zizioulas argues, then obviously they can be without personhood if the traits they are meant to have are missing.[85] Such an understanding is problematic for people with intellectual impairment.

The emphasis on an intellectually based faith has also led to the exclusion of people with intellectual impairments from participating in the practices of the church. John Swinton gives an account of Stephen's encounter with the church. For many years Stephen had lived in institutional care where he showed himself to be friendly and straightforward, passionate about Jesus and a regular and enthusiastic participant in chapel services. Due to the closure of his institution Stephen was expected to move into supported community housing. As his chaplain, Swinton thought it would be a good idea to introduce Stephen to the local church nearest his new home. On their first visit there, Stephen participated in the worship service in his familiar way by calling loudly on "Jeeshuss" on several occasions. Swinton recalls that a representative of the church soon approached asking that "we should either leave or, alternatively, that I should take Stephen through to the Sunday school, where he would be a little less distracting for

---

82. Turner, "Approaching 'Personhood,'" 212–13.

83. See, for example, Turner, "Approaching 'Personhood,'" 212–13.

84. For more on this, see chapter 4.

85. Zizioulas, "On Being a Person," 33. See also Zizioulas, *Being as Communion*, which offers a helpful analysis for questioning Western assumptions that people "have" personhood as opposed to "being" persons. For further reading, see Blevins, "Practicing Self," 23–41; Hicks, "Historical Survey of an Aspect of Personhood," 35–45; McFarlane, "Living on the Edge," 37–50; Motyer, "Physical Community in Hebrews," 235–47; Sheriffs, "Personhood in the Old Testament," 13–34; Starling, "Practical Doctrine of Total Depravity," 10–13.

those who wanted to 'worship in peace.'"[86] Another example involves Justin, a boy living with autism and significant intellectual impairments that rendered him unable to speak. Justin and his family had attended church since he was a baby and, as he grew into his teenage years, made enquiries about Justin participating in communion. His parents reported: "We were initially quite taken aback by what we were told. There was no program or experience with children like him in our parish. A church several parishes away had experience with individuals with disabilities. Initially our (minister) advised us to take Justin there to find out if Justin could be served better at that parish."[87] It was eventually agreed that Justin could meet with the Director of Religious Education to discuss participating in communion at the church. She made it clear that Justin would need to be interviewed like everybody else to ensure he understood what was taking place. Though obviously surprised at the church's intention to question the cognitive capacity of their non-verbal and intellectually impaired child, Justin's parents agreed. During the initial interview Justin made very little eye contact with the Director of Religious Education and "I could tell she was really uncomfortable and unsure of what he understood." Eventually Justin was asked, "What will you do when the [minister] says to you, 'The body of Christ'?" At that moment, Justin "looked directly at the Director of Religious Education and by using limited sign language clearly signed, 'Give Me Please!'" To her credit, the Director of Religious Education immediately commented that she needed no more information, though it is apparent that Justin would have missed out on receiving the care God could provide for him in communion had his parents been less persistent.[88] Another example of this focus on the intellectual capacity to validate participation in communion is related by Swinton:

> At a conference in 1991 I spoke with a Church of Scotland minister whose daughter has Down syndrome. She was a member of the Church of Scotland, and she was a regular attender and participant in worship. He told me that, while in Aberdeen five years earlier (1986), he and his wife and daughter had gone to a city center Church of Scotland for communion. The cup was passed round, but when it reached the handicapped woman, the minister who was administering communion refused to allow her

86. Swinton, *Building a Church for Strangers*, 6–8. See also Berg, "Give Me Please," 181–83.

87. Berg, "Give Me Please," 181.

88. Berg, "Give Me Please," 182.

to participate in the Eucharist. His reason was that he did not believe that she had the intellectual capacity to understand and meaningfully participate in the sacrament. From his theological standpoint, the girl's participation would risk demeaning or even invalidating the sacrament.[89]

At least in this example, the daughter did not have to endure the added indignation of reaching out for the sacrament only to be publicly passed by. Dave Hingsburger recounts the heart-breaking experience of Kerry, a man living with Down syndrome, who every Sunday would make his way to the communion table, and "every Sunday he would be turned away." No one seemed to notice the hurt that showed on Kerry's face caused by this rejection.[90] The reason given by the leader of this congregation for denying Kerry a place at the communion table was that he had Down syndrome and was "unable to understand the content and the mystery of the Eucharist."[91] One might well ask how many typically developing parishioners would be able to truly understand and articulate the depths of its mystery any better!

People living with impairment in any of its classified forms often continue to remain stigmatized by our culture. But arguably, it is people living with *intellectual* impairment who are uniquely "disabled" by our post-Enlightenment Western culture.[92] We believe it is people living with intellectual impairment who are the ones made to sit most awkwardly "on the borders of acceptable humanness."[93] Some have even suggested these individuals are "the other of the other"[94] because of their inability to compete in our hyper-cognitive society. Our society has made it particularly difficult for those living with intellectual impairment to enjoy the type of life, according to *The Universal Declaration of Human Rights*, to which they are "equally and inalienably" entitled.

---

89. Swinton, "Known by God," 142. See also Hingsburger, "First Communion," 173.

90. Hingsburger, "First Communion," 173.

91. Hingsburger, "First Communion," 173.

92. Swinton, *Building a Church for Strangers*, 15–20; Pridmore, "Christian Reformed Church as a Model," 103; Hauerwas, "Timeful Friends," 16.

93. Swinton, "Hauerwas on Disability," 6.

94. Whitney, "Intellectual Disability and Holy Communion," 256. There is a subset within the "other of the other" of persons who have been described as the especially developmentally threatened. See Nielsen, *Are You Blind?*; *FIELA Curriculum*. These are people who have intellectual impairments as well as multiple other disabilities.

2

The Rhetoric and the Reality

WESTERN CULTURES HAVE MADE significant advances in upholding the rights and potentials of people who are living with significant impairment. We want to acknowledge that the work of governments, government agencies, charitable institutions, churches, and many private individuals has made a positive and significant impact on the lives of those living with an impairment and their families. However, almost all the government and agency support take the form of education, therapies, financial help, material benefits, or the provision of paid carers and support workers in a range of situations. While this help has significantly improved the life of the person and their families, it cannot, by its very nature, foster long-term friendships as a normative outcome. Of course, many of these supporters do become genuine friends with those they serve, but in most cases, it is limited by valid constraints around professional boundaries, the caseload to be managed, the length of the support package offered and the demands of their own personal and family life. Even churches can settle for "ministry" as the desired outcome rather than the formation of genuine and long-lasting friendships.

It is here that Jim's personal experience of being a father to children living with intellectual impairment, as well as being a teacher in the Australian education system, led to the decision to interview over twenty five other families (primarily in the Sydney area) about their experiences and how this might inform our more formal academic research.[1] The material that follows is based on a series of interviews conducted by Jim in 2018 and 2019, as well as some of his personal experiences as an educator and as a

1. For privacy reasons we have sometimes changed the location, names and gender of the people interviewed, and at other times we have withheld all the details at their request.

parent. We acknowledge that it is not a statistically valid sample size from an academic perspective, but we believe it offers the same range of stories that would be replicated throughout Australia and other Western nations. Most of the interviews were conducted with people who have a son or a daughter living with moderate or severe intellectual impairment. In some situations, a secondary diagnosis of autism, physical impairment or epilepsy was also present. The aim was simple: to ask these families to talk about their experiences and to hear from them what, if anything, they believed a local church community could do to support their family. Sometimes we share extended quotations in the hope that their position can be more clearly understood by those who have no personal experience of a close relationship with a person living with intellectual impairment or their families.

A Love Like Any Other

> Troy is a very special guy. He has a really positive attitude about life, and he is immensely enthusiastic. He can only see good in people. I can say without any fear of contradiction, that everybody who meets Troy, loves Troy. He is just so passionate about things. Whether it's sports or music—if Troy likes something, he loves it! We are blessed to have Troy. He is my best mate for sure. The journey has been what you would expect—joy at the highest level with a few speed bumps along the way to make you cry, dust yourself off and push forward. More than anyone else in our extended family, Troy's love for and relationship with his family is everything to him. He just wants to be around his mum and brother and me, his cousins, aunts, uncles and so on. I love that connection he has and always will have.[2]

These could be the words of any number of parents talking about their child and the joy that they have from their relationship. They are the words of the father of twenty-five-year old Troy, a young adult who lives with an intellectual impairment. Many of the parents and siblings interviewed emphasized their deep love for and pride in, their son or daughter, brother or sister—and emphasized it was a genuinely reciprocal relationship. One sibling said of their ten-year old brother, "He functions as a fully-fledged family member not as a 'tag-along.' He is forever giving and receiving, he puts music on for all of us, he is a living breathing family member."[3] This

2. Interview 10.
3. Interview 4.

holds true even in the face of severe impairment, and the love clearly goes both ways: "I love my son deeply. He's my boy and I know him like no-one else does. I'm battling hard and I'm fighting hard for him. And he loves me too, maybe because I'm his little comforter who understands things that he knows others will not."[4] Such a love does not minimize the struggles that parents face when their child is diagnosed with an intellectual impairment. Sometimes this was identified before birth, but in many cases, it only became obvious at a later stage. One mother commented: "When Liam was given his diagnosis of intellectual impairment there were a lot of tears shed. But we soon realized that he was still the beautiful boy he had always been. One of his early intervention teachers described him as 'pure sunshine.' And she was right."[5] A father proudly shared: "I am glad he made it through a difficult pregnancy. I am glad that he was born. I am glad that he is here with us now. I'm looking forward to spending as much time as possible together into the future. My son labelled by the world as disabled is one of the best of all imaginable children."[6] The sentiment of that final sentence is not an isolated one. Many of the families interviewed made the point that the love they have for their child is the equal of their love for their other typically developing children. One of the mothers stated: "I absolutely love Jack. When I compare my feelings for him with those for my older son who does not have a disability, well, I get upset even talking about it. I love them both as much as each other.[7] Another stressed that she could not "imagine a world without my boy labelled by the world as intellectually disabled. And I want the world to know—I love him in the same way that I love each of our other children."[8] The same point is made by the mother of thirty-two-year old Noah, a man living with Down syndrome: "Noah is Noah. We love him just the way that he is and just the same as any of our other children."[9] The severity of the impairment does not limit the love. As one father says of his child who barely speaks and who lives with few if any of the skills or abilities that the world says are essential in order to be valued:

> I love him in the same way that I love each of my children. I don't view him as being different. Actually, I don't even really think of

4. Interview 14.
5. Interview 7.
6. Interview 19.
7. Interview 2.
8. Interview 7.
9. Interview 25.

him as having a disability. He is just who he is—one of my favorite people in the whole world to spend time with, a wonderful young fella with his own wonderful little quirks. If I could, I would happily give up work and spend each day with him without any distractions whatsoever. He is worth it.[10]

It appears from the interviews that central to the formation of these strong and deep emotional bonds has been the number and the intensity of shared experiences. One of the inescapable realities of having a child living with moderate to severe impairment is the amount of time one or both parents must spend in medical and therapy appointments. With the child's reduced capacity for independence, there is much more involvement in the every-day routines of life than there would be for a child developing in an intellectually typical way. Both factors lead to much greater parental involvement over a much longer period in a son or daughter's life compared to the situation where a child is developing typically. One mother told of the heart-breaking story of having lived in almost constant fear of her son dying due to the degenerative condition that progressively attacks both his physical and intellectual capacity. For much of his ten-year life span she has fought to keep her much loved son alive. He cannot speak and uses a wheelchair for the often-daily medical, therapy, and school appointments. His condition makes him totally reliant upon her for his all his daily needs. This mother must also meet the understandable and valid needs of their other two children. In the midst of these huge demands, the father works incredibly long hours and is away from home for a number of nights each week to keep the family financially stable. Despite this incredibly physically and emotionally draining life, a life that is in her words often "very chaotic," she still makes sure that there is time each night to shower her son:

> I absolutely love our time together. It is our time. I simply could not give up this very personal routine. I take the time to "cup" him and to massage him with special "breathe-easy" oils. I sit him up, so he is placed over my chest and "thump" his back to help clear his lungs. I have the room so hot with the water and the steam that some nights I nearly faint. Last night he had such a great night's sleep because of all this massaging and "cupping." It makes me so tired, and it means getting behind on everything else around the house, but I simply can't give it up. I love him so much."[11]

10. Interview 21.
11. Interview 6.

The father of Lucas, a seven-year-old living with moderate to severe intellectual impairment, made this same point when he said:

> My feelings for my son are actually growing stronger as we both grow older and as we both get to spend more time together and do more things with each other. He has always had such a very strong connection with his mother who has pretty much always been around with and for him all of his life, especially while I have been at work. My wife has done so much with him and pretty much she has taken him to all of his medical and therapy appointments and early intervention classes. She pretty much always takes him to Primary school now. She is always reading and playing with him. It's not that I never did anything with Lucas, and it's not that he would ever ignore me, but it was really evident that he had a much stronger bond with his mum. Anyway, about six months ago I took a deliberate decision to spend loads more time with Lucas. During a two-week period, I took him to the supermarket shop every single day to buy some grocery items we needed. I took him bike riding at the local park each day on his specially designed bike. I read his favorite books to him over and over again. We daily went for drives to the countryside playing his favorite songs over the car's sound system. A startling thing happened following this period of intense shared experience—Lucas began seeking me out, he wanted to be with me, and I with him. We wanted to be together now, and we had grown much closer. Some of the other kids even joke with their mum now, that Lucas seems to love dad more than her![12]

From the interviews, it was not unusual to hear of fathers having a greater struggle initially to form deep connections with their child.[13] There is an inescapable intimacy in being the bearer of the child, and much of the early care often falls to the mother for a wide range of reasons, but often it is tied to work patterns. When the opportunity emerged and the fathers chose to be involved in a wider range of shared experiences with their child, a deeper and more profound relationship often emerged. It was clear from the interviews that people affirmed the value and worth of their loved one living with intellectual impairment just as they are. They do not require their child to be different in order to be loved or valued.

---

12. Interview 21.

13. For example, Interviews 19 and 27.

The Challenge of Community Attitudes

While families may talk about the reality of their love for their children with intellectual impairment, their experience of life in our community is often very different. Many families suspect that people feel there is something wrong with their child that needs to be fixed. One mother said that she did not like being involved in any conversations that, even unintentionally, would seem to diminish their son. She found it very difficult to handle any talk of their child's limitations or any negative comments about the implications of her role as a mother:

> When a good friend recently said to me "you must have hated missing out on the party because of your need to be at home with . . . " then I immediately felt on edge. It was as though caring for my son might have been a hassle to me. And so, I am really cautious talking about the implications and the complexities of supporting him. I am just so worried that by doing so it might seem as though I would prefer him to be something or someone other than who he is. In some strange way confessing to others the complexities of our situation, seems to risk diminishing him as a person. And if someone thinks I am complaining then I risk seeming as though I have a resentment toward him. That is simply not the case. So, in the end I responded by telling my friend that I didn't mind missing out on the party because I love spending time at home with my son. That is actually true, even though I would have enjoyed attending the party with my husband.[14]

Another mother—her child labelled by the world using the deficit terms "significantly and multiply disabled"—put it very powerfully when she said:

> We've never had any experience where someone's been deliberately malicious, but we have had ignorant people speak to us. Like people speaking in terms of "what's wrong" with our daughter. Saying that there's something wrong with our daughter is difficult for us because it diminishes her. We don't think there is anything "wrong" with her. When people stare and when people make thoughtless comments you just die a little bit as a parent. Even when a kid says it, it hurts. We don't think of Chloe as being "different." She is just who she is. So, when people ask, "What's wrong with her?" I've actually learnt to say, "No, actually there's nothing wrong with her." Her world is more than her disability. There is so much innocence to Chloe. I wouldn't change anything about her

14. Interview 11.

because she would cease to be Chloe, and so she would no longer exist just as she is. We know she'll have hardships, but we just love her just as she is. I know she'll never get married but my son who is typically developing might never get married or might have broken marriages. It's just a society's view about what a perfect life is supposed to look like or how to best define a worthwhile life. But we don't agree with those views. I don't think of her in negative ways at all, even though I realize there are practical implications and challenges to her life and to our life because of her condition. We love and value her just the way she is.[15]

So often people with intellectual impairments are regarded negatively in a society that places a very high value on "making a contribution." The common assumption is that they are incapable of adding any value to the life of the community. Such an evaluation raises questions about our common understanding of contribution. In Western cultures this is too often defined economically rather than socially; furthermore, the value of any economic contribution is often regarded as being of greater worth than any social contribution. The parents interviewed were intent on proudly expressing the contribution of their child to the lives of others. One mother said that there are some limitations and difficulties due to the intellectual impairment experienced by her child, but "My husband and I are constantly surprised by how many kids say 'hi' to him by name just passing through the playground, whether at drop-off, or pick-up, or at special days, assemblies, carnivals, whatever. Kids always start smiling when they see our son. He really seems to have brought joy and happiness to so many of the mainstream kids at his school."[16] Another mother of a teenage boy living with moderate intellectual impairment and autism recounted how her son consistently spends time sitting and mixing with other people who are sick, lonely, or poorly regarded by others. She said that he is "just so beautiful with people who are vulnerable."[17] Even in cases where the community might judge a child as being unable to make a valuable contribution, that does not make it true. A mother of a seven-year old living with multiple and severe intellectual and physical impairments recounts her experience:

We were on a train recently in Melbourne when Chloe met this woman whose appearance was kind of "African American Punk."

15. Interview 13.
16. Interview 11.
17. Interview 15.

> This woman kept looking at Chloe the whole time and eventually Chloe reached out to her. I said to the woman, "Chloe wants to give you a kiss!" As the woman leaned in close enough for Chloe to kiss her, she said to Chloe, "You are so kind." When the train door opened the woman looked back at Chloe and said, "Chloe has made my day." It was so cool to see that a child who cannot talk, who doesn't even have any words, could impact a person in that way. People are drawn to Chloe, and Chloe changes lives for the better.[18]

While some would say parents are naturally biased in their evaluation, their views are supported by the comments of others. One man said:

> My nephew is a young man living with intellectual impairment. His parents are so proud of the contribution he makes to the lives of others. My wife and I think they have got good reason for that pride. When he comes to our place, he plays non-stop with our young kids for the duration of his two or three-day visits. I can't think of anyone who is better at interacting with our kids. Some may be his equal, but no-one is better. For his whole time with us he plays indoor and outdoor games and sports with our kids and just basically hangs out until he is an absolutely spent force. We love that he values our children in this way, and each of our children really love him too.[19]

Challenges Do Exist

It is important to recognize that life with, or as, someone living with intellectual impairment can often be difficult. The love witnessed and expressed through the interviews is a love that exists amid these challenges. Kirk Patston has written:

> I have deliberately paid attention to the ways that disability is not a problem that needs a solution. But I don't want to sound like a shallow optimist. My experiences of disability have come from my work as a therapist, from being the father of a boy with intellectual impairment, and a girl whose disability meant she lived only briefly. Close contact with the lived experience of disability can mean we find the stories, beliefs and clichés of our culture a little thin—unable to help us live with, or as, a person with a disability. I have shed my share of tears. . . . So, while I have tried to be positive

18. Interview 13.
19. Interview 19.

about disability, I don't want to be unrealistic or sentimental. . . . Disability is difficult.[20]

In writing this book we are aware of the dangers of being shallow optimists and presenting only the positive side of living with intellectual impairment. It is true that love, cooperation, unity, and joy often abound in families where impairment is present. It is also true that it is often difficult, impacting marriage and sibling relationships, causing emotional and physical exhaustion, as well as bringing safety concerns in the present and fears for the future. It usually has significant financial and time implications, as well as radically altering employment opportunities and career aspirations. The families that were interviewed for this book were remarkably candid about those pressures, even admitting that at times they became "totally infuriated with their child and with the situation of their impairment."[21] Another person confided: "Living with a severely disabled person, being a parent to them, is all the hard work without the same level of reward. Because of the complex nature of our child's condition, our story will not head in a trajectory of 'getting better.' It's probably going to get worse. In general, we have little heartbreaks every day, we mourn to a certain extent what our daughter's life could have been like."[22] One parent confided that she wished she had a different son to the one she had.[23] Even persons living with intellectual impairment report difficulties and challenges as part of their life. Like their parents or key carers, these challenges sometimes involve frustrations with the impairment itself and the implications it has for their health and opportunities in life. It can involve frustrations in the formation, development, or maintenance of relationships. For example, during the course of one interview with a young man, he reported his frustration that his intellectual impairment was restricting his ability to live independently, form and maintain a longed-for romantic relationship and was therefore restricting his ability to have children of his own in the future. He made the rather poignant comment, "I don't like having epilepsy either."[24]

We decided to quote from two interviews at length to show just how difficult it can be dealing with the myriad pressures arising from caring for a

---

20. Hurley, *Take Heart*, 8, 12.
21. Reference withheld for privacy reasons.
22. Reference withheld for privacy reasons.
23. Reference withheld for privacy reasons.
24. Interview 8.

daughter or son living with moderate to severe intellectual impairment. The mother of Oliver spoke at length about some of her family's challenges:

> When I compare our life with Oliver to that with his older sibling, I see just how much more complex it is to support Oliver. The main difficulty is that we find it extremely difficult to access the community. Oliver is too strong for me now. If we go to the shops, there is a very real possibility of his having a meltdown or him running off somewhere. And it's just a trail of people continually looking at us and turning around to see what the noise is. And there is this desperate desire that so many people seem to have to give you parenting advice. It seems like people get this urge they cannot resist to give you advice even while your boy is still having a meltdown. And when Ollie is yelling out in a really loud voice, you get a certain look that communicates an opinion that I should be controlling and disciplining him. . . . People . . . rarely seem to want to offer any help. Then there's this deep sense of loss at not being able to do what people typically do. You can't go to the movies because he runs off, you can't go to the park on your own because he might run off . . . you just can't access the community without substantial help.
>
> Then of course there are many times when it's chaos at home. We are continually adjusting our situation to try and improve it. . . . We've had to put locks on every door, locks on the pantry or he'd be in there all day, or if you wake up in the morning everything would be out of the drawers . . . we have big-time security outside where we have locks for all external gates. There are also locks for doors to get from the inside to the outside. There's always that notion of "locking." We've just got to be so very careful with his safety and it's kind of like we are under lockdown constantly—we simply have to "Oliver proof" the house. Everything has to be up high otherwise everything kind of gets wrecked. . . . Ollie's sister really misses out. She goes inside of her room and locks herself in with the lock on the inside of the door. She is a nine-year-old girl who has to keep her special things locked inside of her room because otherwise they would get wrecked.
>
> And our parents on both sides are limited because of their age. So, they really can't help. Perhaps we could leave Oliver for an hour or so every now and then with one set of parents but that that would be the extent of it. Even that is becoming more difficult because he is now too strong and too fast for them as well. Friends have offered help sometimes, but we don't feel it is fair to use those friends too much. And even our close family on

both sides are busy and we accept they've got their own lives. So, we do feel a bit isolated.[25]

The mother of Liam and Lucas identifies "an ever-changing revolving door of complexities":

> Some are constants that will potentially always exist as long as our boys live. Safety for example. The boys are always going to be more vulnerable than our children who are developing typically. Therefore, my husband and I will always be concerned for their safety—whether that be because we worry that they themselves don't perceive unsafe situations like roads, cars, strangers, or that others will take advantage of their vulnerability. So, their safety is a constant complexity as it prevents either the boys individually, or us as a family, from participating in a range of activities. It also means that our normal everyday home-life looks very different to the "normal" of most others. We have very structured, two-adult procedures in place both to leave the house (load the car, get the kids safely into the car and buckled up, check that nothing in the house has been fiddled with, left on or is overflowing) and to return home again (negotiating the transition back home, often tears/meltdowns, safely getting everyone from the car into the house, getting the car unloaded and locked up and making sure the house doors are locked behind us once we are in.
>
> We have recently decided to trial taking the baby gate off the entrance to the kitchen. . . . The baby gate has been such a peace-of-mind safeguard, meaning we haven't had to worry about our boys getting their hands on a sharp knife, or turning on the taps and flooding the kitchen floor, or popping an expensive mobile phone into a kitchen sink full of water, or playing with the buttons on the dishwasher until it breaks, or touching a hot element on the stove, or turning the gas on the stove without one of us realizing . . . you get the picture.
>
> There are other issues such as neither boy being able to regulate how much they eat, or how quickly they eat, or whether they put too much into their mouth at once risking choking, having free access to the fridge which contains quite a few glass receptacles which smash when dropped (as do plates, bowls, glasses etc.). The kitchen became such a stressful nightmare to all of us that gating it off was a very welcome relief. The stress dissipated quickly once that gate went up. Of course, children grow taller and wiser and we've realized the gate is not really cutting it anymore—the kids are starting

25. Interview 14.

to step right over it. So, the trial of its' retirement has begun. To say we are on-edge would be an understatement.

Our front doors are always dead locked with the keys kept out of the way from all of our kids. I can't even put into words adequately the stress that exists around the potential for our boys to get out that front door. They have zero road-safety and a very dangerous fascination with running onto the road. I want to cry even just thinking about that possibility. But now one of our kids has worked out that if he gets a chair, he can reach the keys even though they are at the very top of the door frame. And so, the trials and the adjustments continue.[26]

In spite of the incredible challenges, parents will often return to speak of their love of, and their pride in, their child. Liam and Lucas's mother says of her two boys that she loves them "more than life itself" and of how "where there are storms, there are also rainbows."[27] Oliver's mum speaks of her love for "my boy" and of her pride at the "special way" that only she has to communicate with her non-verbal son.[28] Other parents who spoke about the complexities and the regrets of their situation, also returned to emphasize their love for their child. Several shared about their deep and ongoing fear of who would look after their child once they were gone. A father spoke of the joy at such shared experiences as going for long walks using the stroller, going to the shops, or playing at the local pool. He spoke in very protective terms of his deep pain that his daughter will never have the joy of marriage, and of the injustice when people walk into the room and say hello to everyone else except his daughter. Without doubt life can be difficult for each of the persons involved in a family where intellectual impairment is present, including for the person living with the impairment. As one mother puts it: "Yes, there are plenty of challenges, plenty of hard days, and plenty of tears but look at my son, look at who he is, look at what he does for others—what a beautiful way to be."[29]

Many parents shared their ambivalence at times regarding the possibility of changing some aspect of their child's condition if they could. They love their child just as they are and just for who they are, but for most there are aspects of their child's condition they would change if that change was clearly in their child's best interests. One mother declared: "I wouldn't

26. Interview 7.
27. Interview 7.
28. Interview 14.
29. Interview 15.

change William. Not for my sake anyway. I mean I'd want to take some challenges away from him for his sake, but his essence and his soul are so beautiful just as he is."[30] This is echoed by Ryan's mother: "I don't want Ryan to change. If he didn't have all his traits, then he would cease to be who he is. I love him just as he is, and I certainly don't want to change him for my sake. If I thought a change could make things better for his sake, then I would like to make that happen for him. But not because I need him to be different."[31] Even siblings report the same sentiment: "Cure? Why would there need to be a cure? Even if there was one, I wouldn't want them to get it. I like my brothers just the way they are."[32] The families interviewed were insistent they did not want others to pity them because their son or daughter lives with an intellectual impairment. The father of Jack, a ten-year old labelled as having moderate intellectual disability, autism and moderate physical impairments, explains:

> Before my early forty's when we had our son, I remember meeting people who had disabled kids and thinking "that must be terrible for them." I would have expected to have felt devastated, but I don't feel that way. I occasionally do think that life is a little unfair and I've been saddled with this, but I don't generally feel that way. When you have a son with a disability, apart from the fact that it was a slow and creeping realization for us, you don't feel like, I don't know, how would you describe it, you don't feel like you've been cheated or anything like that. Because you realize very early in the piece that he's your kid and you just kind of feel like it is normal. And now, having had the experience of living with and loving my own son, I have come to realize that feeling dreadfully sorry for that friend of mine who had a kid severely affected is an un-natural response. I can see now that my friend just loved her, and loved looking after her, and so you realize now that his love and approach was just perfectly natural for him.[33]

30. Interview 15.
31. Interview 16.
32. Interview 20.
33. Interview 3.

Better Never to Have Been Born?

A mother of a teenage girl living with multiple and severe intellectual and physical impairments once confided in Jim that no-one ever described her daughter as being beautiful, "not even when she was born."[34] This mother has experienced the heartbreak that her much loved daughter is not valued by our culture in the same way as other typically developing children. She is by no means alone in this experience and many families report how this feeling emerged through an interaction with a person or organization. Some families first encounter such an evaluation at the stage of prenatal testing:

> When Chloe was still waiting to be born, we had this really difficult meeting around the twenty to twenty-two week mark in the pregnancy. We were encouraged to have an amniocentesis with its risk of having a miscarriage. But we'd already had a miscarriage, so we weren't going to do that. Then a Professor comes in and tells us we'd be better off terminating the pregnancy because "it" is not going to be normal. And I said, "Well what's normal?" and the Professor says, "Well you know, she won't have all of her legs and all of her arms and she'll have other complications, so you are better off with a termination." And we said "No, that's not an option for us." . . . So, he sent us to a genetic counsellor. She was nicer than the Professor but still we were asked if we wanted to terminate. We again said "No." We just didn't like it at all. And when we came out of that room, we could see another couple crying because the husband wanted to get rid of their baby and the mum did not.[35]

In due course they were blessed with a much loved and beautiful baby girl. Some had indicated to her parents that it might have been better if their daughter had never been born. After her birth she was labelled, from the very beginning, using a negative construct—she was "severely disabled." The devaluation of Chloe by some in the medical field has continued over the years: "There were some within the medical world who gave no indication whatsoever that they even saw Chloe as a real person. It was like she was just a case file that was a hundred pages long. A long list of comments and details on paper. These have been some of the worst, most heart-breaking interactions I have experienced over the years. I find it hard to revisit

---

34. Conversation with a parent. Reference withheld for privacy reasons.
35. Interview 13.

those types of interactions."[36] Is it any wonder then that the memories of that initial prenatal interaction with the Professor can still bring tears to the eyes of Chloe's parents? The recommendation for a termination was based on the medical evaluation of the potential quality of life—Chloe would never live "a normal or worthwhile life."[37] This medical evaluation is routinely offered to prospective parents when the baby has been diagnosed with Down syndrome, Fragile X syndrome or a range of other conditions. One mother said this was the first option offered to her when the doctor shared the results of her screening test. She reflects:

> What if they chose to encourage and inspire rather than default to the option of termination? . . . Individuals with Down syndrome deserve to be celebrated, to be valued, to be accepted and to be loved. They are amazing people, full of love, and capable of so much if given the chance. Not a day goes by that I don't look at my son and feel so grateful I chose the option to love, accept and believe in him today and every day.[38]

While a number of the families we interviewed spoke about their positive encounters with the public and private education systems, this was not, sadly, everyone's experience.[39] Several of the parents shared stories of the devaluation made by some in the education system, even if unintentionally. While not denying there were challenges in having their child at school, people confessed their hurt at the outcome for their child. One father said:

> Henry started off at school at one place and they did the best they could for him but from the start they were very limited. The hardest thing for us was finding out that Henry just hid out in the sports cupboard during lunchtime because he didn't have any friends. He didn't know how to socially interact—but there was not any support offered for his social interaction either. He just had to battle his way through the jungle as best as he could and that hurt us. That was hard. During that year we asked at a parent-teacher interview where our son sat in the classroom. She said, "He just sits over there in the corner," and she pointed to a petitioned-off area. He had remained there for a whole term sitting on his own and left to his own devices.[40]

36. Interview 13.
37. Interview 5.
38. Binger, "'Options' Parents Need."
39. For example, Interviews 11, 15, and 18.
40. Interview 18.

A mother shared her struggles from the days of mother and baby groups, to day care to primary school. For example, at pre-school her daughter was not permitted upstairs with her same-age cohort, even though there was a wheelchair lift capable of transporting her to that location. When they applied for a placement at several local schools when she turned five, the family was told there was no place available. Instead she was made to wait until her daughter turned six, a point at which the education system could no longer legally deny her a placement. The family made an obvious and heart-breaking assumption from these events that the system did not value their daughter in the same way as a typically developing child. The mother concluded by saying: "We understand that she's got limitations, but we just don't want people to put their limitations on her. Our daughter is an awesome person who wants what we all want: to feel loved, to be valued, to belong and I wish people could see that more easily."[41]

Sadly, the situation was generally far more depressing for families who enrolled, or tried to enroll, their children in non-government (mainly Christian) schools. One father mentioned the challenge when trying to enroll his child living with moderate intellectual impairment in the local Christian school. The Principal of the school was happy to take their older typically developing child, but "explained that they were a parent-controlled Christian school and that the parent body didn't want to be known as the school in the local area that took students who were like our son. It just wasn't the kind of 'feel' the parent body wanted for the school."[42] A mother reports asking a range of Christian schools to enroll their son living with an intellectual impairment and getting a negative response from all of them before finally managing to enroll him in a private school for children on the autism spectrum. She acknowledges the issues around funding for children with particular needs in the private system:

> But in the end I'm just not sure that they really want to be involved. Special Education just does not seem to fit within the parameters of what they want to be involved in. I mean they can find millions of dollars for new sports fields, swimming pools and so on, but, in the end, they don't want to be involved with my son Ollie because he has a disability. I think the other parents

---

41. Interview 12.
42. Interview 19.

don't want to have "those types of children" in their schools because they see them in negative terms.[43]

She went on to say, "It's just feels like you have to beg all the time. You have to fight for things that other parents simply take for granted, things like education."[44] This mother also noted that things were not much better when trying to attend church for a special service for World Autism Day. They were made to feel really uncomfortable because of their child's autistic behavior: "I found it really difficult that the church couldn't accept my child just as he is and that hit hard. . . . I just thought to myself 'Why the hell did I come here? Why the hell did I put in all that effort?' I just thought, 'I don't think you guys know what we're going through.' We ended up by going outside."[45]

Sometimes a negative evaluation is offered by other family members, friends, and even strangers. The language of "what's wrong" with your child immediately diminishes them, even if there was no malicious intent. Sometimes people speak in terms of the importance of avoiding the risk of having another child who might be impaired like the one they already have. Seth was diagnosed at two-and-a-half years of age with autism spectrum disorder. The parents took nearly three years to embrace that reality and then decided to try for another child. They recount how concerned family and friends kept asking if they wanted to take the risk of having another child like Seth.[46] Seth's parents interpreted this line of conversation to mean that these people felt the world would be a better place without him. It is similar to a comment made to some parents at an extended family Christmas party: "Well, you chose to have him!"[47] On another occasion a family's much-loved child was described as "an absolute nightmare" by a close relative.[48] Admittedly, many of these comments are made without any intention of causing offense. The people who make these comments will often declare their love for the person and are genuinely surprised and mortified to discover they have brought pain to those involved. However, the parents interviewed consistently affirmed

---

43. Interview 14.
44. Interview 14.
45. Interview 14.
46. Reist, *Defiant Birth*, 123.
47. Interview 28.
48. Interview 29.

that these unwitting comments cause deep and ongoing hurt and remain a stumbling block in these relationships.[49]

For some, the sense of devaluation emerged with the realization there were no social invites for their child from people outside of their immediate family. One mother tells how she felt supported by the staff at her child's preschool, "but the parents were terrible because they would invite everyone in the class to a party but not my son William. . . . Then there were times when people would invite his younger brother but not him. And I found that really hard . . . the times when people looked down at us in the shops, the 'tut-tutting' in church when William would make a noise, these were the hardest times."[50] The end result of all this was to "sort of drift away and you don't really become part of the group because your child is so different."[51] It is this perceived sense of "difference" that hurts so many parents. One father of a young girl living with multiple and severe intellectual and physical impairments has noticed:

> It is not uncommon for people to come into the room and say hello to everyone else but not to my daughter. It's like she is not even there. That is probably the most hurtful thing—no-one really wants Sofia, she hasn't got any friends, she'll never have any friends, and she'll never get married. I think we would like people to make special trips just to see Sofia. But no-one makes a special trip to see Sofia. People might make a special trip to see one of her brothers, but no-one makes a special trip to see Sofia.[52]

Sometimes even the extended family makes things difficult:

> I have two children and sometimes there's a Friday night when it's cold and raining. And there might be a movie on TV. Anyway, one of my extended family will ring and they'll invite my eldest (who is typically developing) to come over and watch the movie and even to have a sleepover. But they don't offer that to my son with a disability. And I think to myself "well what about Ryan?" And so, my eldest will get to go out for the movie and the sleepover, but Ryan won't be given that same chance. . . . Once or twice in the past decade, one of my extended family members has rung up and said they felt bad at spending time with his older sister but not with him. They feel bad about it and so they invite him over. But

49. Interviews 6 and 29.
50. Interview 15.
51. Interview 15.
52. Interview 1.

it's more out of a sense of obligation than desire. But we wanted it to be about desiring him, about valuing him.[53]

Finding and keeping a job can also prove to be a demeaning exercise. Australia's national television broadcaster, the ABC, recently aired a documentary series entitled *Employable Me Australia*. In it, a documentary team traced the experiences of people living with a range of intellectual and physical impairments as they searched for work. Marty is forty-five and lives with a genetically acquired intellectual impairment known as Fragile X: "I'm looking for a job and I want to get the best job I can possibly get. I am a punctual, hard-working guy. I've never been late in my life. I am a really happy guy. I'd be good with customers; I love helping people." Marty has all these wonderful characteristics and is good at keeping to routines and operating equipment but in an almost thirty-year work life he has only had a few, brief jobs. Sinead lives with Down syndrome and reports, "I've been looking for a long time, but they don't want me. I don't know why. People treat me as though I am a kid. I want to be treated like the adult that I am." Many other cases were covered in the series, and all of them were battling to show employers that their differences could prove to be a strength for their organization. It is little wonder that so many of them give up in the face of the constant rejection. Kiah, for example, is about to give up: "I'd like to have a job so that I can use my strengths and abilities in ways that will let me feel productive. I am prepared to take anything I can get, but I've been knocked back so many times that my social worker just told me to stop looking for a job and apply for the pension instead. In the end, in terms of job hunting, I just end up setting the bar really low, so if something good happens from there then it is a bonus." Even when the person has been able to demonstrate solid achievements in a range of volunteer positions, the transition to paid employment is still difficult. Jake, who is in his mid-twenties and lives with an intellectual impairment and epilepsy, has volunteered successfully for many years in his dad's mechanical repairs workshop. He has shown an ability to address a whole range of mechanical issues and is currently restoring a stretch limousine by himself. His dad said that he gets a real sense of achievement from the job, and just needs someone to give him a start and when Jake misses out on a job he always asks, "Why me dad, why me?" With the help of professional advocates, psychologists, job coaches and their families, some of the people in the series have been able to secure employment. Others have been unable

53. Interview 16.

to find work and are continuing their search for the meaning, the validation and for the sense of contributing that having employment can bring. Rohan summarized the situation well when he said, "I would just like to be treated normally. I don't just want a job; I need a job. It is not a 'want' for me, it is a 'need' for me. . . . We all have the duty to contribute to society. I want the chance to do that, to be treated normally, equally."[54]

People with moderate to severe intellectual impairment can also have their life evaluated negatively at the point of their death—even if these evaluations are not intended to offend or cause pain to the immediate family. One of the interview respondents spoke of the many premature deaths he had encountered involving young people who had lived with severe intellectual impairment and additional health concerns. In the weeks following these funerals the suggestion that everyone was now "better off" would commonly be made. There was a clear perception that the premature death of someone who was significantly impaired might well come as a relief to everyone else because of the difficulties and hardships experienced by the family. The typical comments included: "I know how much they loved their daughter, but life must have been so impossibly difficult for the family," or "He was a great kid but it's probably for the best," or "It wasn't really much of a life, was it?" Such comments imply that this was a life that had never really been worth the living in the first place. The comments also suggest that this person's death may well have been gladly received by the rest of the family because it finally frees them from the burden of their existence. This may not have been the intention of the people making the comments, but it is certainly possible their words will be received this way. It is a telling exercise to compare the comments made following the premature death of a typically developing person with those made following the premature death of a person who has lived with severe and multiple impairments. This final devaluation adds to a long line of devaluations that have at times been applied to this person's life all along.[55]

Meaningful Relationships

Troy's family has spent considerable time laying the groundwork to develop friendships for their son by introducing him to local sports, recreational

54. O'Clery, *Employable Me*. Excerpts are drawn from episodes throughout the series and from the follow-up program, "Where Are They Now?"
55. Interview 19.

and church organizations. Troy does very well in his relationships within his family and is doing particularly well with the sporting connections that he has made in the community. Unfortunately, things did not work out quite so well at the church group. His mother takes up the story:

> We did try a church youth group and Troy really enjoyed this. As a younger person this was fine but when he outgrew the younger youth group activities the next step was a young adult Bible Study. This was intellectually not suitable for Troy. We had hoped he would form friendships, but relationships never progressed beyond that hour or two of the Youth Group or Bible Study. We really wanted friends and relationships to develop for Troy that extended beyond the time of the programmed group. This didn't eventuate. There just seemed like there was nowhere to go after the group outgrew him intellectually.[56]

The family's hope was for Troy to enjoy real friendships beyond the hour or two of the programed group. Families and people living with intellectual impairment need real relationships, not simply ones that are timetabled to occur at given times when the program is running. Many of the families we interviewed expressed this same need. They agreed that you cannot force people to be a friend but they continued to hope for people to form a genuine friendship beyond any expected behaviors due to the setting (for example, school, sports group, youth group). Parents would like to see others develop an affection for their child just for their own sake. One father said: "I just want people to like him, I want him to make friends, you want him to be likeable and liked, for his own sake. I know sometimes he can be challenging to be with. Most people seem to shy away from friendship with someone who is harder to understand or apparently harder to get along with."[57] This strong desire for friendships was very evident when speaking to the father in another family situation. He indicated that their primary concern in choosing a school for their son Henry was the possibility of friendships emerging within that environment. Even though as a family they recognize and value the importance of an academic education "the social aspect of school life was our primary concern."[58] At his previous school, Henry "simply didn't have any friends—and what we really wanted for him

56. Interview 9.
57. Interview 2.
58. Interview 18.

was to have friends." Henry recently graduated from the school and his dad concludes the story by saying:

> If you ask Henry, and if you ask us, what was the single greatest thing that Henry has got out of being involved in his schooling life then the answer is simple—it is friends. It's interesting now because he now has exactly what his older sister has—a real core group of friends. Long-term relationships are really important. We want him to have relationships where he is valued for who he is and also for what he brings to the table and the contributions he can make.[59]

Henry's family is certainly not alone in their view about what was most important from school life. A highly experienced consultant in the field of Special Education, explains that the most important thing for families is for their child to be seen as a person. Part of that affirmation of personhood is seeing their child getting the opportunity "to take part in things that are considered normal" and the first and foremost of these "normal things" are friendships. "So many parents say to me 'I never thought my child would have a friend!'" The consultant explains that this is why invites to birthday parties are so important. They serve a dual purpose. First, it helps the young person feel a part of something and gives them the opportunity to form friendships organically outside of the programed school environment. Second, families need these invites "almost more for them than their child" because "it allows them to see their child with a disability is accepted by others, is liked, and that they were considered worthy of being invited."[60]

This desire for meaningful relationships remains true in family situations regardless of the level of intellectual impairment. Even in situations where severe and multiple impairments are present, families still know and affirm their child as a person of dignity and worth and as someone capable of giving to others. Many years ago, in Jim's role as a teacher, he enjoyed a conversation with the mother of a much respected and valued teenage student who had been in his class for several consecutive years. This student lived with a range of severe and multiple impairments including intellectual impairment, life-threatening epileptic seizures, regular upper-respiratory infections, and blindness. She was also unable to walk, to talk, or to make deliberate movements on many occasions. Because this teenage student loved hydrotherapy (which also had many benefits), Jim and the team

---

59. Interview 18.
60. Interview 16.

that supported her arranged for multiple weekly swimming sessions in the school's hydrotherapy pool. The young lady's mother would often come to school during these times and she would take the role of standing beside the pool and "spotting" for safety, while Jim would remain in the water to facilitate the hydrotherapy. On one of these occasions, as her much-loved daughter floated on her back with her neck and head resting on Jim's shoulder as he stood behind her, she commented how much her daughter liked Jim. Jim asked how she knew this to be the case. She replied that it was the way her daughter relaxed her body and deliberately moved her left cheek in to nestle against Jim's right cheek as she floated on her back with her legs stretched out in front. That one simple and deliberate gesture communicated a profound reality. Parents in these circumstances know the communication techniques being used by their children and this mother knew that her daughter trusted Jim and was responding and engaging with him in significant ways. In this simple gift of her trust and affection the student, evaluated so negatively by many in our culture, was providing Jim with a gift that he still remembers fondly more than a decade later.[61]

Families, with good reason, are often deeply hurt when people make little or no effort whatsoever to enter a relationship with their child. The father of a young boy with significant and multiple impairments spoke during the interviews about the times when people come into the room and do not even acknowledge the existence of his son. Instead he remains in the room without receiving a greeting or an interaction of any kind.[62] Another father has also noticed a decreasing tendency for people to relate to and interact with his daughter as she has grown older. He is not sure why.

> There was someone who was very good with our daughter at first—cuddled her lots, gave her lots of attention, she just loves attention, was very attentive. But gradually, over the years, this person is not so good anymore and I just don't know why. Maybe she is a bit bigger and more difficult to hold. This person is not terrible at interacting, they are still one of the better ones with our daughter but gradually they have become less good. Most people are not very good at interacting. Most people are either five out of ten for attentiveness to our daughter or somewhere between zero and five. But very few people would even be five out of ten or better using that scale. In the end I think that is probably the most hurtful thing about this whole situation. . . . No-one seems

61. Reference withheld for privacy reasons.
62. Interview 1.

to really want our daughter. She hasn't got any friends and I don't think she ever will have any friends.[63]

Discovering what matters most to young adults with intellectual impairment has been an interest of Jim's for almost twenty years of teaching in this age group. Just before the graduating class of seventeen and eighteen year old students leave school for the last time, Jim has asked them: given three options of (a) a good friend, (b) a meaningful job, or (c) indulging in their favorite hobby, what would they most value as they move into post-school life? Each year the answers have always been the same—more than two-thirds of students respond that they would most value having a good friend. Even those who say they would prefer a meaningful job, almost always include as part of their reason that a job would help them to find friends. Some students are perfectly happy and content to keep their own company or the company of their immediate family, but even they often indicate having ongoing, meaningful friendships is still important.[64] This desire for personal friendship is so strong that some people living with intellectual impairment will go to extraordinary lengths to try and foster a relationship. Jim shares how a young man living with Down syndrome would make fun of one of his long-term friends who also lived with an intellectual impairment whenever a certain group of typically developing young adults was around. On each occasion the young man was acting out of character. When Jim asked the young man with Down syndrome why he did this, he replied with tears streaming down his face, "I thought I could make friends with the group by saying something that would make them laugh. And so I made fun of my friend because I just want to have more friends." And with absolute honesty and sincerity, he went on to emphasize his point by repeating, "I know it wasn't the right thing to do, but I really just want to have more friends!"[65] This heart-breaking story underscores how important it is to initiate and then foster a greater number of genuinely joy-filled, mutual friendships between people of all intellectual abilities.

---

63. Interview 1.
64. Interview 8.
65. Reference withheld for privacy reasons.

Conclusion

An analysis of the interviews has highlighted that two issues stand out above everything else as being of major importance to people living with moderate to severe intellectual impairment and their families. The first was the desire for other people to value and affirm the person living with impairment as someone with inherent dignity and intrinsic worth. It seems such an obvious thing to say but it is just so damaging to the person and their family when people say or imply that they are mistakes, are not as fully human as the "normal" person or are of less value than others. In the Western world, the dominant medical paradigm is to see someone living with an intellectual impairment as less than a person and the decision regarding their quality of life is so often made from that particular perspective—leading to the offer of a termination prior to birth. While the education, church and charitable institutions often try to make life as rich as possible for those living with impairment and their families, they usually operate on a service model, even if delivered with love and compassion. This cannot meet the vital need expressed by the families, and the persons themselves, for genuine friendships between people of all intellectual abilities. The social isolation experienced by people living with an impairment and by their families is very real and is destructive of their well-being. It is often true that we only try to form friendships if we believe it will be worthwhile, mutually beneficial, and enriching. If we harbor doubts about the capacity and competence of the person then we will usually pass them by. It will take a deliberate choice to foster a friendship with a person who lives with intellectual impairment. For this to happen we need a different understanding of what it means to be a person than the dominant paradigms we meet with in our Western culture. If genuine relationships are to be formed, we need to be grounded in a different model of being fully human.

3

What Does It Mean to Be Human?

As we have seen from the interviews, one of the major concerns raised by families where there is a child with moderate to severe intellectual impairment is the way that other people view their deeply loved child. Granted that such persons with the impairment may have difficulty with communication, physical co-ordination, and mobility, many in the wider community struggle trying to relate to someone with these limitations, and some even question their personhood. With the current emphasis on genetic testing to eliminate known "defects," the rise of legalized euthanasia and the demand for assisted dying when life is no longer adjudged to be worth living, many families who have a child living with intellectual impairment sense that their son or daughter is no longer valued or wanted in our society.

Peter Singer, the Australian philosopher and ethicist, is on record as advocating that babies up to four weeks of age have no right to life, and he is not referring here to severely impaired babies. He asserts that babies are not "rational," they have no awareness of their own existence, and so cannot be described as a person.[1] In Australia euthanasia is now legal in Victoria and Western Australia, but the conditions that must be met are tied to an incurable condition that will be terminal within 12 months. This would not have allowed Australian scientist Professor David Goodall to end his own life at home, and he would still have needed to travel to the Dignitas clinic in Switzerland, as he did in 2018. In an interview he said that it was his choice to make as he dealt with the realities of his own declining abilities and its accompanying loss of dignity.[2] The loss of dignity is

---

1. Franklin, "Lethal Philosophy of Peter Singer," 1–8. The key work is Singer, *Practical Ethics*, esp. 135–217.
2. "Australian Scientist Offers Last Thoughts."

often described in terms of incontinence, immobility, inability to shower, dress, or feed oneself, the loss of speech, and being reduced to an apparent vegetative state. Imagine how this makes families who have children with severe intellectual disability feel, let alone the children themselves? This makes it even more important for us to carefully consider what it means not just to be a human as a biological organism, but what it is that makes us a person. Across the centuries both philosophy and theology have given a range of answers to the question. Since the period of the Enlightenment modern science has increasingly added its own specialist understanding. This has given Western societies three major views concerning the definition of human personhood: biological anthropology, philosophical anthropology, and theological anthropology.[3] Clearly, the view you hold on humanity/personhood directly impacts how you treat other human beings. Certainly, philosophical anthropology lends weight to the notion that some human beings are worth more than others.[4] It illustrates the danger of tying personhood to a list of certain characteristics or qualities. What happens if these are absent—do we then become non-persons as Peter Singer suggests? In the rest of this chapter we briefly explore three major ways of defining humans and personhood.

A Biological Anthropology

A biological anthropology essentially views humans as just one animal species amongst many others, and it takes a strongly Darwinian approach to the survival of the fittest. It is also a materialistic view and tends to see humans as objects. One of the well-known advocates of this viewpoint is Richard Dawkins, who developed a whole explanation of our current existence in terms of the human genome. Dawkins can be regarded as the first, and still the most systematic, ethologist of the gene. This stance claims that it is the human gene that drives all human behavior, and it operates to maximize survival and the passing on of the genes to the next generation. There is no "design" behind all this, it is simply the survival of the fittest. Everything can be explained by chance mutations over long periods of time and human behavior is nothing more than the physical manifestation that results from the encoded genetic instructions.[5] Closely related to this genetic

3. See Evans, *What Is a Human?*, 1–23.
4. See Evans, *What Is a Human?*, 173–90.
5. McGrath, "Ideological Uses of Evolutionary Biology," 329–51.

perspective are the developments to be seen in modern neuroscience. The recent explosion of knowledge about brain function has impacted human self-understanding in profound ways. Linked to these developments and associated with the development of computers and Artificial Intelligence, the human brain has often been compared with digital computers. They both "contain a large number of elementary units—neurons and transistors, respectively—that are wired into complex circuits to process information conveyed by electrical signals. At a global level, the architectures of the brain and the computer resemble each other, consisting of largely separate circuits for input, output, central processing, and memory."[6] It has become common to compare the physical brain to the hardware, and the mind to the software. In such a model, some would claim that we are preprogrammed by a range of biological factors to act in certain ways.

This perspective, that we are simply a biological computer, with no real ontological distinction between the artefact and the living being, is shared by a large number of physicists, biologists and philosophers.[7] This is clear in the claim of absolute biological determinism, and

> one of the most influential forms of this at present is neurological determinism. Of course, the brain is involved in every aspect of human functioning. Except in the most basic reflex-like reactions, it is not bypassed. However, there is a strong form of neurological determinism that would go further and say that our emotions, thoughts and personalities are "nothing but" what goes on in our brains, that we are "just a bundle of neurons" as Francis Crick put it.[8]

The popular reporting of discoveries in the neurosciences regularly offer to the public accounts of the mechanisms behind thinking, loving, and choosing. While the scientists themselves may place careful limits on their claims, this is rarely made obvious in the press accounts.[9] This reporting creates the impression that our genes and physiology "seem to be controlling us, so we can't even change our mind."[10] They are often seen as a blueprint or instruction manual, linking a gene with specific behaviors,

---

6. Luo, "Why Is the Human Brain so Efficient?"

7. Burdett, "Image of God and Human Uniqueness," 8–9. See also Lumbreras, "Strong Artificial Intelligence," 157–68.

8. Watts, "Multifaceted Nature of Human Personhood," 57.

9. Hogue, "Brain Matters," 50.

10. Alexander, "Genes, Determinism and God," 1.

emotions, attitudes or motives that are beyond any conscious control.[11] "Human behavior and what it means to be human are therefore completely determined by our genes. All behaviors, including our religious and artistic impulses, are simply reflections of some survival advantage for a particular section of DNA."[12] This has the effect of making us little more than biological machines and so we can be treated as we treat any other machine. If it is malfunctioning, then we either repair it or discard it.

Many reputable scientists would argue that science does not require us to accept an inescapable, genetically programmed determinism. There are other ways of understanding personhood that do not require us to accept strong reductionism (that we are nothing but a collection of random interacting molecules). They reject the belief that "all of the causal forces in human mental activity and behavior can be accounted for on the basis of neurophysiology, neurochemistry, and ultimately physics."[13] In a 2010 paper Stuart Judge notes that strong reductionism undermines the concepts of free will, moral choice, responsibility, and culpability. He writes that "our knowledge of neurons and their structure presupposes the general validity of our conscious experience and reasoning. That we are able to make valid observations and reason about them cannot be less certain than the conclusions of those activities." He points out the absurdity of neurons claiming they are nothing but neurons.[14] Even if it were possible to describe the neural mechanisms that underly every aspect of human experience, that still does not mean that human freedom or human consciousness are illusions. The description of the process does not necessarily capture the experienced qualities of conscious experience.

While modern technology allows us to observe and study the physiological and electrochemical processes of the brain, "the entirety of human experience, meaning-making, and identity cannot be reduced to electrochemical firing patterns. In other words, while the brain and mind are inexorably linked, the self-reflective and self-transcendent quality of the 'mind' is somehow different than the 'brain.'"[15] It is clearly possible "to find

---

11. Alexander, "Genes, Determinism and God," 2.

12. Hewlett, "What Does It Mean to Be Human," 153. See also McGrath, "Ideological Uses of Evolutionary Biology," 331–32.

13. Brown, "Nonreductive Physicalism and the Soul," 1816.

14. Judge, "Nothing but a Pack of Neurons," 2. See also Flaman, "Neuroscience, Christian Theology," 252–56.

15. Roozeboom, *Neuroplasticity, Performativity, and Clergy Wellness*, 44.

neuronal activity that *correlates with* the cognitive performance" but this does not solve the question of causation.[16] Many scientists and philosophers point out that "the neurological story is always essentially incomplete because the brain is not the whole person."[17] The data of human experience are in a different realm of discourse from those of neurophysiology: "Thought and perception are predicates of an agent rather than a piece of hardware."[18] Subjectivity is outside the scope of pure science, yet subjectivity is essential for human interaction (friendship, love) and humans value the subjective states of others as much as their own. "The moral implications of ignoring the importance of subjectivity endanger the core of what it means to be human . . . freedom and responsibility are ultimately based on consciousness, so that finding a functioning ethics without these concepts would be a considerable challenge."[19] It is only as conscious agents that we are able to design the experiments, make the observations and interpret the results that lead us to our neuroscientific conclusions. The mistake in strong reductionism is not in the positive assertion that we are embodied in neural machinery, but in the denial that we are anything else.[20]

A strong reductionism often sounds persuasive in academic papers and popular presentations of their findings, but the social realities of persons are neglected. Our brains are not isolated organs living in a laboratory, they are an essential element of persons living in a culture. The culture and social relationships play a very significant role in how the brain organizes its information into systems and behaves in response to that information.[21] So, while evolutionary psychology showed that viewing "the mind as a kind of software running on the brain's hardware can advance our understanding of the origins of human cognition . . . it's time to take a further step: to recognise that our distinctively human apps have been created by cultural, not genetic, evolution."[22] This is a clear move from a mechanistic model of the brain to an ecologically centered, systems-based view. We are embodied beings. The brain is not a computer that executes genetically predetermined

---

16. Judge, "Nothing but a Pack of Neurons," 1.
17. Midgley, "Consciousness, Fatalism and Science," 30.
18. Judge, "Nothing but a Pack of Neurons," 1–2.
19. Samuelson, *Artificially Intelligent*, 163.
20. Judge, "Nothing but a Pack of Neurons," 3. See also Samuelson, *Artificially Intelligent*, 254; Lumbreras, "Strong Artificial Intelligence," 162.
21. Hefner, "Imago Dei," 79.
22. Heyes, "Cognitive Gadgets."

programs—we are actively involved in its development. The field of neuroplasticity concerns itself with the brain's dynamic malleability and "while genes or biological makeup is important, it is not deterministic and we do have the ability, and responsibility, to shape our brains in life-giving ways. Our practices and experiences have the power to reshape and rewire our brains, and our identities . . . brain function and behavior mutually inform one another in a two-way process."[23] That means that our thinking ability is built in childhood through social interaction, and fashioned by cultural, not genetic, evolution.[24] The debate over the relative importance of nature or nurture creates the impression that human personhood is fragmented and that there is an existential battle between these two forces for dominance.[25] We can define determinism in its hard form as the thesis that "given our particular genome some elements of our lives are not really up to us, including certain apparent choices." There is also a softer form of genetic determinism which states that "given our particular genomes our lives are more likely to follow one particular future."[26] The latter form is not incompatible with free will as it simply states that all our lives are circumscribed by a range of circumstances of one kind or another. Dennis Alexander says that in terms of free will: "There is nothing in contemporary behavioural genetics, barring some severe psychiatric pathologies ascribable to mutant genes, that render the reality of that experience less plausible."[27]

A Philosophical Anthropology

Philosophical anthropology distinguishes between the human being as a biological entity and the human person, and it is personhood that is morally and ethically significant when it comes to determining the qualitative status of the human being. This is not only the domain of pure philosophy, but also the philosophical framework that shapes how scientists interpret the data they observe. In this view, the findings of the biological sciences are generally accepted to define humans as a species but a simplistic identification of the biological creature with personhood is disputed. Both philosophers and scientists then operate with a list of personal and social traits that identifies

23. Roozeboom, "Rethinking Theological Anthropology," 79.
24. Heyes, "Cognitive Gadgets."
25. Alexander, "Genes, Determinism and God," 2.
26. Alexander, "Genes, Determinism and God," 2.
27. Alexander, "Genes, Determinism and God," 4.

personhood as a distinct reality alongside the biological markers of the human being. The content of such lists of traits varies, but in Western countries for the past five hundred years or so the "predominant model of agency in terms of which our flourishing is conceived, and to which dignitary status is attached, is one highlighting self-sufficiency, independence, a capacity for deliberation and rational transcendence of emotion—that is, effective self-determination and self-control."[28] As a result, certain human beings will not count as persons and they will not be seen as morally significant. This would certainly include the unborn and the newly-born, some of the very elderly, and those with intellectual and developmental impairment—people who have not yet developed or have lost the capacity for conscious reflection.[29] Human dignity is tied closely to our capacity for reason and personal decision-making resulting in independent action.[30]

The recent debates on euthanasia have highlighted again the question of what it means to be human, and whether there are situations in which personhood is not present even if biological life is. One of the most influential voices in these debates is the philosopher Peter Singer. He is a Professor of Bioethics at Princeton University's Center for Human Values, and the University of Melbourne's Centre for Applied Philosophy and Public Ethics. His key book, *Practical Ethics,* has been translated into fifteen languages and is used in courses throughout the world. He believes that the "life of a newborn baby is of less value than the life of a pig, a dog, or a chimpanzee is to the nonhuman animal."[31] He goes on to argue that "life only begins in the morally significant sense when there is an awareness of one's existence over time."[32] Building upon these views, Singer proposes the notion of the replaceable fetus/newborn baby in cases where disability is detected, since neither the fetus nor the newborn baby is aware of their existence and they are not to be considered as a person. Consequently, he reasons that it is feasible to abort the unborn child with disabilities or kill the newly born child with disabilities on the basis that the loss of their life "is outweighed by the gain of a better life for the normal child who will be conceived only if the

---

28. Carse, "Vulnerability, Agency, and Human Flourishing," 35–36.

29. Thompson, "Christianity," 3. That is why someone like Peter Singer can claim that infanticide is morally acceptable, as is euthanasia.

30. See Kleinig and Evans, "Human Flourishing, Human Dignity," 554–55.

31. Singer, *Practical* Ethics, 122–23.

32. Singer, *Practical Ethics,* 189.

disabled one dies."[33] Singer explains: "When the death of a disabled infant will lead to the birth of another infant with better prospects of a happy life, the total amount of happiness will be greater if the disabled infant is killed. The loss of a *happy* life for the first infant is outweighed by the gain of a *happier* life for the second. . . . Killing a disabled infant is not morally equivalent to killing a person. Very often it is not wrong at all."[34]

In 1996 Singer defended two sets of parents who wanted their newborn infants with Down syndrome to die. He explained:

> There is no sharp ethical distinction between what they did, and what most pregnant women do when they are offered an abortion because the fetus they are carrying has Down's syndrome. . . . There remains however the problem of the lack of any clear boundary between the newborn infant, who is clearly not a person in the ethically relevant sense, and the young child, who is. In our book *Should The Baby Live?* my colleague Helga Kuhse and I suggested that a period of 28 days after birth might be allowed before an infant is accepted as having the same right to life as others. This is clearly well before the infant could have a sense of its own existence over time, and would allow a couple to decide that it is better not to continue with a life that has begun very badly. . . . Could we return to a view of infants more like that of ancient Greece, in which a public ceremony a short time after birth, marked not only the parents' decision to accept the child but also society's conferral on it of the status of a person?[35]

For Singer, an individual should not be deemed as a person until they demonstrate rational capacity and a sense of their own existence, and not before those involved with them recognize they are capable of contributing happiness to others, and enjoying happiness themselves, in ways equivalent to any potential replacement child. Peter Singer continues to hold and argue for these views through to the present day. While many would reject the strong views Singer holds, there are many others in our society who share the sentiment. In a society that values independence, self-reliance and personal choice, people living with mild to severe intellectual disabilities are at risk of being considered as lesser persons or less than persons, even though they would still be regarded as biologically human.

33. Singer, *Practical Ethics*, 188.
34. Singer, *Practical Ethics*, 186, 191.
35. Singer, *Rethinking Life & Death*, 217.

The popularity of this view does not do justice to the incredible richness and complexity of human life. It also raises the issue of the minimum threshold of whatever the determining trait is—how much rationality, autonomy, etc., and is there a hierarchy of traits? Questions about the quality of life are then raised in the midst of these considerations. A person's quality of life is usually defined in terms of physiological or psychological functioning and once this drops below a certain threshold, the person is adjudged to have minimal to no quality of life. This is, of course, a judgement exercised by people with a particular definition of what a normal life looks like and then making assumptions about the quality of life of those outside their benchmarks. It can lead to decisions that some lives are not worth living because they have no net positive value or significance as determined by an influential sector of the society.[36] If personhood is largely defined by rationality, then the absence of (or loss of) cognitive power is clear evidence of a diminished or non-existent quality of life. In a society that values being in control and being independent, persons with severe impairments who are dependent on others are evaluated negatively: "Our attachment to impoverished paradigms of control and self-determination in human life diminishes our potential to join others in meaningful forms of connection essential to human flourishing."[37]

A Christian Theological Anthropology

There is little dispute regarding our understanding of a human as a biological creature, the differences come when we seek to define personhood and how this is related to biological existence. The dominant Western views stress either a substantive definition of personhood, in which we possess some qualities or traits that define our essential personhood. In the West, this is largely seen in terms of reason, logic and autonomous decision making. This perspective is usually accepting of physical impairment if there is nothing more than mild intellectual impairment present. In most cases, the person with a physical limitation can still function intellectually and therefore can be regarded as a full person—think of Stephen Hawking. The functional view looks towards the ability of the person to contribute to the overall welfare of the community and generally accepts a degree of both physical and intellectual impairment as being compatible

36. See Wyatt, "Quality of Life."
37. Carse, "Vulnerability, Agency, and Human Flourishing," 47.

with personhood. The challenge comes in both cases when a human life fails to measure up to their minimum standard of acceptable intellectual or physical functioning. The danger is that the biological human being ceases to be a person. The current debates over both pre-natal testing and euthanasia center around this acceptable minimum and when the human fails to meet that, or falls from that due to accident, disease or ageing, then they never were a person, or are no longer a person. No one disputes that human beings are clearly biological creatures, but that is not all they are—they are special to God in ways that other life forms are not. Exactly what makes them special is where the debates arise. This is where a theological anthropology offers a very different understanding.

If we see personhood as something we have, then it is tied to the willingness of others to recognize our personhood by judging whether we have certain capacities and capabilities. For persons with any form of impairment that is clearly problematic because they may not be seen to exhibit those qualities in a sufficient manner. From a Christian perspective, our understanding of the nature of human beings is foundationally located in God's revelation to us through the Person of Jesus Christ, Scripture, and the long tradition of the church. The definition of personhood commonly centers on the biblical claim that we are made in the "image of God" (*imago Dei*). This has enabled Christian theologians and philosophers to explore other dimensions of our personhood. The *imago* (explicitly mentioned in Gen 1:27; 9:6, but also referenced in Rom 8:9; 1 Cor 11:7; 2 Cor 4:4; Col 1:15) has been commonly described in terms of three major models: functional (dominion over creation, stewardship of the earth); substantive (some quality or faculty inherent in humans, often the capacity to reason); relational (with God and other humans).[38] For some Christians, the preference has been the substantive model, especially our rationality. This picture, as we saw earlier, has found much support in the scientific community. The danger here is the tendency by some theologians to reduce or eliminate God's transcendent presence within the natural realm, which makes it difficult for the natural sciences alone to deal adequately with questions relating to the meaning and purpose of life.[39] However, while accepting that we are rational creatures, many Christian thinkers argue that this is not all we are. They would argue that this narrow view of humans as "independent, autonomous, choice-making beings" is inadequate

---

38. Herzfeld, "*Imago Dei/Imago Hominis*," 8. See also Burdett, "Image of God," 4–5.
39. McGrath, "Ideological Uses of Evolutionary Biology," 340–41.

and unnecessarily limits personhood to those displaying a certain range of traits. We are not just a collection of attributes in which the loss of one or more of them diminishes our personhood. The functional model, as its name suggests, locates the essence of the image in our ability to carry out certain tasks. These are usually associated with our abilities to shape our environment for human purposes. The problem with both the functional and substantive models is that when a person is incapable of exercising the function or exhibiting the trait, do they then lose the image? That is why we need to provide a model of what it means to be human beyond our current focus on rationality or functionality.

Thomas Noble reminds us that any reflection on what this means must take account of the nature of the God in whose image we are created.[40] Trinitarian studies are a vast and complex field but all orthodox Christians confess that the One God who created us and whom we worship is truly Three Persons—Father, Son and Holy Spirit. The Nicene Creed affirms that the three Persons of the Trinity are distinguishable from one another, are in an eternal unbroken communion with each other, but still one Godhead. The question arises as to how they relate to each other, what lies at the core of their tri-unity? In a landmark study, Noble demonstrates that is it one of the greatest of the early Church theologians, Augustine, who explicitly identifies that it is love that lies at the heart of the relationships within the Godhead.[41] Augustine's understanding of the purpose and goal of human life is clearly centered on love:

> Reason shows us that happiness, our acknowledged goal, requires the love and possession of the best that human nature is capable of achieving. This perfection of our higher nature must have an eternal pattern or objective to pursue, which can only exist in God. The authority of Scripture confirms what reason tells us, for the great commandment is, "Thou shalt love the Lord thy God with all thy heart, with all thy soul, and with all thy mind." Happiness is to be found then by pursuing God, that is, by loving him. We are able to pursue him because we already have a revelation of the Triune God. Paul, who tells us that the love of God is in Christ Jesus our Lord, also tells us that the love of God is "shed abroad in our hearts by the Holy Spirit who has been given to us." So virtue proves to be nothing but the perfection of our love for God. Temperance, courage, justice and prudence are simply different forms of love.

40. Noble, *Holy Trinity, Holy People*.
41. Noble, "East and West," 368–70.

> The second great commandment is to love our neighbour, and this is a stepping stone to the love of God. And since love for God is the pursuit of our *summum bonum*, then only he who loves God may be said to love himself truly.[42]

As we mentioned earlier, Zizioulas has argued that for too long now it has been assumed "that people 'have' personhood rather than 'being' persons."[43] This is why the third option, the image as primarily relational, is so important. It defines personhood within a framework of the unconditional love and acceptance by God rather than by intellectual capacity or functionality. "A rich theological anthropology provides guidance on how to . . . find meaning in the vulnerabilities that accompany birth, aging and its developmental challenges, acute and chronic illness, and dying."[44] It seeks to uphold the vital importance of our social nature and its implications, along with a proper consideration of our human finiteness and limitations (illness, disability and death) in a creature striving to transcend these limitations.[45] It is a model that finds surprising support from the work of many in the social neuroscience and psychology fields.

> Social neuroscience strongly affirms the *essential relatedness* of human beings. A wide range of studies document the critical role of the interpersonal environment in shaping fully functioning human brains. A focus on individual brains, encased in individual skulls, developing from a strict genetic code, is increasingly hard to defend. . . . Prior to the development of language, and probably even prenatally, critical social pressures interact with genetic instructions to shape the human brain, for better and for worse. We are conceived, nurtured prenatally and born in relationship and we are nourished by human connections throughout life. There is a very real sense in which the soul exists only in its connection with other souls.[46]

The neurosciences remind us that there are "invisible processes of life"[47] that lie beneath our conscious awareness that enhance our ability to relate to one

---

42. Noble, "East and West," 368. It is this view that profoundly shaped John Wesley's understanding, as we shall see below.
43. Zizioulas, "On Being a Person," 33.
44. Taylor, "Health Care and a Theological Anthropology," 226.
45. Hamel, "Health Policy and a Theological Anthropology," 234–5.
46. Hogue, "Brain Matters," 44.
47. Hogue, "Brain Matters," 47.

another and remind us of "the intra/inter-relationality of human persons."[48] A central component of such a Christian anthropology is that to be human means to be in a relationship with God, with one's self, and with other human beings. This is underscored by the Creation account in Gen 1–2. In Gen 2:18 we read that it was not good for the human to be alone, even though he had a deep personal relationship with God and could enjoy the presence of a vast range of animals. And so, God determined to "make a helper suitable for him" (Gen 2:18b). With regard to this verse, Claus Westermann has commented: "There can only be anything like humanity and human relations where the human species exists in twos. . . . A human being must be seen as one whose destiny is to live in community; people have been created to live with each other."[49] To be alone and without human companionship was not then, and could not be now, a good thing.

A Wesleyan Theological Anthropology

John Wesley affirmed that human beings were created by God with both a material and a spiritual element (see Gen 1–2). While this can easily be read as a form of Cartesian dualism, it is important to understand that these two elements were essentially interdependent: "it was ordained by the original law that during this vital union neither part of the compound should act at all but together with its companion; that the dependence of each upon the other shall be inviolably maintained; that even the operations of the soul should so far depend upon the body as to be exerted in a more or less perfect manner, as this was more or less aptly disposed."[50] Human beings are biological creatures and as such share much in common with other living creatures (particularly the great apes). However, only human beings are described in Scripture as being made in "the image of God." Wesley asserted that the *imago Dei* can be understood in several ways. In his sermon, "The New Birth," he says:

> "And God," the three-one God, "said, Let us make man in our image, after our likeness. So God created man in his own image, in the image of God created he him." Not barely in his *natural image*, a picture of his own immortality, a spiritual being endued with understanding, freedom of will, and various affections; nor merely

---

48. Roozeboom, "Rethinking Theological Anthropology," 1.
49. Westermann, *Genesis 1–11*, 160.
50. Wesley, *Sermons*, 4:296.

in his *political image*, the governor of this lower world, having "dominion over the fishes of the sea, and over the fowl of the air, and over the cattle, and over all the earth"; but chiefly in his *moral image*, which, according to the Apostle, is "righteousness and true holiness." In this image of God was man made. "God is love": accordingly man at his creation was full of love, which was the sole principle of all his tempers, thoughts, words, and actions.[51]

It is evident that in this description there are points of agreement with both the substantial and the functional models. Thus the natural image indicates that we are capable of reason and culpability, while the political image speaks of our function as the stewards of God's creation. However, the moral image is essentially about sharing in the character of God: "And what is righteousness but the life of God in the soul, the mind which was in Christ Jesus, the image of God stamped upon the heart, now renewed after the likeness of him that created it? What is it but the love of God because he first loved us, and the love of all mankind for his sake?"[52]

As we see, the value of reason (substantive) and obedience (function) are clear, but "without love all learning is but splendid ignorance, pompous folly, vexation of spirit"[53] for it is love that is the essence of the *imago*: "His [Adam's] affections were rational, even, and regular—if we may be allowed to say 'affections,' for properly speaking he had but one: *man was what God is, Love*. Love filled the whole expansion of his soul; it possessed him without a rival. Every movement of his heart was love: it knew no other fervour."[54] In one of his many explicit statements on this identification of God's image being fundamentally love, he says:

> For to this end was man created, to love God; and to this end alone, even to love the Lord his God with all his heart, and soul, and mind, and strength. But *love is the very image of God*: it is the brightness of his glory. By love man is not only made like God, but in some sense one with him. . . . Love is the health of the soul, the full exertion of all its powers, the perfection of all its faculties.[55]

---

51. Wesley, *Sermons*, 2:188.
52. Wesley, *Sermons*, 1:481. See also Wesley, *Sermons*, 1:495, 579.
53. Wesley, *Sermons*, 1:175–76. See also Wesley, *Letters*, 26:564–65.
54. Wesley, *Sermons*, 4:294 (emphasis mine). This is a major theme in 1 John, with 4:8, 16, being explicit that "God is love."
55. Wesley, *Sermons*, 4:355–56 (emphasis mine). See also Wesley, *Sermons*, 1:184, 581; 2:439. He does refer to the image in several ways: natural (which includes reason), moral and political.

Furthermore, it is the love of God for us that initiates the relationship—we love, because he first loved us.[56] This is underscored in his understanding of the nature of salvation as a relationship of love restored: it is "the revelation of Christ in our hearts: a divine evidence or conviction of his love, his free, unmerited love to me a sinner; . . . I know he 'hath loved *me*, and given himself for *me*.'"[57] All of this emphasizes Wesley's deep conviction that the focus of the creation narrative was the relationship between the Creator and the human beings he made, not any ontological qualities that humans possessed. This relationship is defined by love, which he believed is God's essential nature,[58] and this lies at the heart of his whole theological framework. It is equally clear that this strong emphasis on love and relationships "suggests that the image of God is not something we possess, but something we experience; we are in the image of God when we are in authentic relationship with God or with one another."[59] Since God always initiates the relationship, no one will ever cease to be a person: "God gives all his children a significant identity by knowing them, regardless of the limitations they might bear."[60] The constraints of living with moderate to severe intellectual impairment and the subsequent limitations of being able to fully express this love received, cannot affect the relationship with God, which transcends the experience of physical existence. We are unceasingly "remembered" by God,[61] and "to be remembered within God's love emphasises that God's grace, love and mercy are not dependent on who we are or what we have done, but are simply there for us. God has taken the initiative and it is enough that the person just be as they are. This is prevenient grace."[62]

For Wesley, the essence of the image of God is tied to God and God's love. Its origins lie in our creation, as we are created by love for love. The initiator is the Creator and not the creature. The Bible makes it plain that God loved us before we had experienced love for ourselves or could return it to him. Because it begins with God and his love, it does not rest on any

---

56. Wesley, *Sermons*, 1:481. See also Wesley, *Sermons*, 4:377. The scriptural basis for this is very clear in 1 John, particularly 3:1; 4:10, 16.

57. Wesley, *Sermons*, 1:405.

58. See Wesley, *Sermons*, 1:225–35, 348–50. See also Wesley, *Sermons*, 1:204–5, 225–35, 348–50; 2:188; 4:294–95, 377.

59. Herzfeld, "*Imago Dei/Imago Hominis*," 48. See also Brown, "Nonreductive Human Uniqueness," 98.

60. Rosner, *Known by God*, 201.

61. Goodall, "Caring for People with Dementia," 253–54.

62. Goodall, "Caring for People with Dementia," 255.

qualities, traits, characteristics, or abilities that we might possess. There are certainly elements in our biological makeup that make us living creatures, but none of them frame what it means to be a person from a Wesleyan perspective. It is the originating love of God that forms our potential, capacity, and inclination to love in return. It is critical to understand that all are loved equally by God, even if all cannot express or return that love in obvious ways due to a range of physical, intellectual, and emotional limitations. We are all special to God and to diminish one person, for whatever reason, is to diminish all. Western culture is thoroughly inconsistent in its evaluation of human worth. For example, in the field of education intellectually gifted students are lauded for their achievements, talented sports people are acclaimed, and the artistic have their work displayed. They are all "special" and celebrated as such. The people who do not fit into these categories are usually overlooked, and this is even more evident the further away from the successful intellectual, sporty, or artistic paradigm you are. We appear to celebrate and desire some types of difference but not others. Before God, people with different levels of intellectual function remain special, equal, and essential in their difference. A person living with moderate to severe intellectual impairment is not a "sub-optimal" person, they are as complete a person as anyone else, even if they cannot express their personhood through our usual evaluative mechanisms of intellect, speech, and function. Christine Bryden, in sharing her personal account of living with dementia, notes, "Such love does not need me to behave normally or consistently; it does not need me to know who you are, or even who I am. We bear with one another in love. Dementia is a disability that, to you, may seem to erode my personhood, so it is all the more important for me to be held in communion with you. In this way, my personhood exists in relationship with you and with the divine."[63]

As we noted earlier, this devaluation at the hands of sympathetic family, friends and professionals probably originates in the ongoing prevalence of attitudes that are tucked away in phrases such as "handicapped person," "disabled person," or "impaired person." This framing of personhood often leads to the charity model with its tendency towards condescension. For many people who live with an impairment, this "charity model" can quickly become problematic when it is adopted uncritically by a church community. As Mike Duggan points out, the core problem is that it all

---

63. Bryden, "Spiritual Journey," 11–12. See also Bryden and MacKinlay, "Dementia," 69–75.

too easily leads to a "one up, one down" mentality.[64] In this situation the church community fill the role of the host (the "one up") and people with an impairment fill the role of the guest (the "one down"). The host will often create specific events (such as special church services or special fellowship outings) that the guests attend. This process tends to disengage the guest from the choice-making process, confining them to their group and excluding them from participating in the ordinary life of the church and its people. Far from encouraging the development of genuine relationships between people of all abilities, such well-meaning hospitality can reinforce the "us" and "them" mentality. It can become a form of "spiritual apartheid" where there is "a separating out of people with disabilities from society and the congregation."[65] But this does not need to be the norm. The church *can* have a more God honoring engagement with people who live with an intellectual impairment. We could choose instead to see God in the position of host and all of us together as his guests. As Duggan says, "we are all in this boat together . . . and we all share a common humanity."[66] The church community that recognizes these theological realities is far more likely to ensure that *all* people (including people living with an intellectual impairment) have the opportunity to enjoy God and his hospitality as well as the opportunity to share in relationships with others that are characterized by love, reciprocity and equality. Without this, it is unlikely that they will develop genuine friendships with those who have a moderate to severe intellectual impairment.

Conclusion

As we will see in the next chapter, the measure of our personhood is not in our current demonstration of these qualities, traits, characteristics or abilities, nor is it our capacity or inclination to return the love we receive from God. It lies wholly in the love God has for us and the potential we all have to respond, even if the full actualization of that awaits a post-resurrection life. We are unable to evaluate what will come to flourish in any human life because we are not God. We are the objects of divine love and, as finite creatures, we can never exhaust the lavish resources of the infinite Creator

---

64. See Duggan, "Implications of 'Special' Church Services"; "Reflections on My Life"; "Theology of Disablement."

65. Duggan, "Theology of Disablement," 2.

66. Duggan, "Reflections on My Life," 7.

who has chosen to love each one of us fully and equally—no matter how we ourselves evaluate personhood. Just as God does not love some more than others, neither does he regard some as more of a person than others. It is this perspective that says to all those currently living with impairment, their families, friends, and carers that the God who spoke the first word of love, is the same God who continues to speak words of love for time and eternity. This indicates that the person living with an impairment is a person in the fullest sense of that word, even if there are severe physiological and intellectual impediments to a full expression of that personhood. The limitation does not lie with their personhood, but with our willingness to recognize and acknowledge them as full persons, and to love them as we would anyone else that we regard as a full person. The sad reality for many living with moderate to severe intellectual impairment is that other people demonstrate attitudes and practices that subtly indicate they don't really think this is a person in the fullest sense, and certainly not to the same degree as others who are developing typically. Even though many genuinely well-meaning people would argue intellectually that they see someone with a moderate to severe intellectual impairment as a person, it is another matter for them to consistently affirm and interact in ways that reveal that this is a person to the same degree as every other person. Certainly, most family members and friends (and hopefully most Christians) would not say the intellectually impaired are non-persons, but they often seem to behave as if they are less of a person, leading to the types of devaluations parents spoke about in the interviews.

The assumption made by those who have typically developed intellects is that they are the measure for those who do not. A Wesleyan theological framework (and indeed most other Christian theological frameworks) insists that it is not a matter of some being at 100 percent capacity then being able to devalue someone else at 70 percent, 50 percent, or 30 percent capacity, because we are all, in some way or other, impaired. Theologically there is no comparative or relative scale of impairment before God. We are, *each one of us*, impaired without qualification. If we would be offended by being labelled as a non-person or a depleted person due to our own impaired state, should we not also be offended when that designation is given to people living with moderate to severe intellectual impairment?

4

The Image of God: Broken and Being Healed

THOSE WHO HAVE TYPICALLY developed intellects (and bodies) are used to seeing themselves as normal and everyone who displays any diminished capacity or capability is described as "impaired." The assumption being made is that they are the measure (100 percent) for wholeness and everyone else is then assigned a description that fits their self-chosen framework. So, a person with 80 percent intellectual capacity is mildly impaired, someone with 60 percent is moderately impaired, and someone with 20 percent is severely impaired. The assigning of the descriptor is made with reference to an agreed norm, even if various experts in the field have a slightly different scale. A Wesleyan theological framework (and indeed most other Christian theological frameworks) insists that as humans currently exist, no one is at 100 percent in either capacity or capability. This is true even for the healthiest persons because the impairment is not simply linked to observable bodily, intellectual, or emotional health. As Jurgen Moltmann has observed: "Every human life has its limitations, vulnerabilities and weaknesses. We are born needy, and we die helpless. So in truth there is no such thing as a life without disabilities."[1] That means that we are all, to some measure, impaired and therefore no one can operate from a position of superiority, making judgements about the personhood of those who, by their measure, are less than whole.

All the major traditions of the Christian church in their doctrinal confessions believe that humans were created by God completely whole, both in terms of capacity and capability. There was no physical, mental, emotional, or spiritual impairment (the implications of Gen 1–2). Equally, all major Christian traditions accept that something went wrong (best described in

---

1. Moltmann, "Liberate Yourselves," 110.

Gen 3:1–13) that negatively impacted the whole race. The details of both realities are heavily debated, as are the details of how the life, death and resurrection of Jesus Christ has provided the solution to the problem.[2] Given the focus of this book is on personhood and friendship, there is no intention to engage with the theological complexities of the doctrine of salvation as such. Rather, we want to reflect on how the life, death, and resurrection of Jesus and the gift of the Spirit provides healing and the restoration of the person (*imago*) and enables the reestablishment of friendships. We also need to consider what are the limitations to this healing here and now and what potential is still to be realized post-resurrection. It is to an examination of this from a Wesleyan perspective that we now turn.

Human Impairment

As we saw earlier, at the heart of a Wesleyan understanding of the image of God is love and relationships, with the other perspectives on the image relating more to our biological existence as creatures. The first humans freely chose to listen to the voice of the tempter, ceased to fully trust God and thereby damaged their relationship with him, and consequently their relationship with each other and the rest of the creation. Robert Lawnton has described the content of Gen 3 as a "series of reversals."[3] These reversals occur in several ways, but all have to do with relationships, which are clearly central to God's creation of humanity. The damaged relationships are between humanity and God; the human beings themselves; the humans and the animals; humanity and the environment. Essentially the whole of Gen 3 is concerned with describing the disruption that had occurred to the loving, equitable relationships that had been established *and* described as the focal point of the previous two chapters. The theological term that is most used to describe the impact of this on humanity is "sin." Wesley said that the consequence of human sin was that the image of God (understood relationally) was now "effaced."[4] He firmly believed that our bodies and souls are interdependent, and what impacts the one also impacts the other. Because the human race had rebelled against God, the seeds of weakness, sickness and

---

2. Any standard introductory theology text covers this. From an evangelical perspective, see Bird, *Evangelical Theology*; from a specifically Wesleyan perspective, see Collins, *Theology of John Wesley*.

3. Lawnton, "Genesis 2:24," 98.

4. Wesley, *Sermons*, 4:354.

death are "lodged in our inmost substance—whence a thousand disorders continually spring, even without the aid of external violence."[5] The consequences of this rupture with God and with each other had an impact on the physical body—it was now "corruptible"[6] and that would lead to weakness, sickness, pain and finally death.[7] He graphically described this in terms of disease: "Our nature is distempered, as well as enslaved; . . . Our body, soul, and spirit, are infected, overspread, consumed, with the most fatal leprosy. We are all over, within and without, in the eye of God, full of diseases, and wounds, and putrifying sores."[8] This "disease" has now impacted every life since and it disrupts all our relationships. One of the consequences of this in so many Western societies is the increase in loneliness, which is destructive for physical and mental health, not just the social isolation itself. There is solid scientific evidence demonstrating the importance of having high-quality friendships for increased well-being and general health.[9] This has obvious implications for people with intellectual impairment and their families who reported in our interviews struggling to make and then retain friendships beyond the immediate family circle.

The Genesis passage also makes it clear that the rest of creation was negatively impacted by the human decision. Instead of being faithful stewards of God's creation, human beings would now misuse and abuse the creation for their own selfish ends. The consequences for both human beings and the planet result in an ever-increasing amount of damage to the person, the community, and the environment. This leads to forces of destruction impacting every human life in ways that are impossible to exhaustively trace or to which we can always assign a cause and effect sequence. Sometimes human choices do result in relational, physical, and mental damage that can be traced, but in most cases they cannot. In terms of intellectual impairment, it is possible to trace some conditions to genetics, problems during pregnancy or childbirth, illness, or injury. These may involve personal choice, social structures, environmental and biological impacts. In very few cases is it possible to link a single choice with a single cause that directly results in an impairment; in many cases, there is no obvious cause at all. Even when genetics are identified as the cause, that still does not necessarily identify

---

5. Wesley, *Sermons*, 32:110.
6. Wesley, *Sermons*, 2:405. See also Davies, "Loneliness Is a Modern Scourge."
7. Wesley, *Sermons*, 2:477.
8. Wesley, *Sermons*, 4:354.
9. See McEwan, "Whose Body, Whose Life," 47–70.

why a parent has that genetic code. All this is to say, that from a Wesleyan perspective, while the initial root cause of our current reality is clear, the actual cause or causes thereafter are beyond our ability to fully unravel. The critical point in all of this is that life as it now is cannot be regarded as the norm for determining human value.

The Healing

Wesley (like most Christian thinkers) was convinced that our current damaged existence was never God's intention, but it was always a possibility for creatures who genuinely had the power to choose, who could reject God's love but then had to live with the consequences that flowed from their choice. Because of the decision to no longer live in love and harmony with God, we are all born into a world ravaged by the consequences that have subjected all of us and our environment to corruption, dysfunction and disorder. The damage of sin can be understood by reference to guilt or shame, needing forgiveness and reconciliation. For Wesley, as we saw above, it can also be thought of in terms of disease that requires healing.[10] We need to be clear that he does not literally mean that sin is a disease, but that it acts like a disease, in that it has "infected" every human being since the account in Gen 3 and that infection corrupts and destroys human flourishing. It is only because of God's great love for the human race that he did not abandon us to the consequences of our choices. The remedy God provided was a physician who can "cure" the disease. Jesus Christ is the great Physician to heal our diseased souls: "Know your disease! Know your cure! . . . By nature ye are wholly corrupted; by grace ye shall be wholly renewed."[11] The healing (salvation) provided through Christ shows us an "amazing display of the Son of God's love to mankind."[12] Salvation is therefore to be thought of primarily in terms of being restored to the image of God in which we were created.[13] He was equally confident that God's intention was to restore us "to the whole image of God"[14] understood in

---

10. Wesley, *Sermons*, 4:196–99. On Wesley's therapeutic understanding, see Maddox, *Responsible Grace*, 73–83.
11. Wesley, *Sermons*, 2:185.
12. Wesley, *Sermons*, 2:427.
13. Wesley, *Sermons*, 3:200. See also Wesley, *Sermons*, 4:293–303.
14. Wesley, *Letters* [Telford], 4:88–89.

relational terms.[15] Wesley is certain that "love is the health of the soul, the full exertion of all its powers, the perfection of all its faculties"[16] and in it we exchange "bondage for freedom, sickness for health."[17] The focus of the healing (salvation) is principally about re-establishing a relationship of love with both God and the neighbor, though in due course all of the creation will be renewed.[18]

This offer of healing is made to every single human being and the basis for it is simply God's nature as love, not any qualities or capacities that we might or might not have. Wesley is in no doubt of the absolute fixity of God's love for us and that "the grace or love of God, whence cometh our salvation, is free in all, and free for all."[19] It emphasizes that God's love cannot, by its very nature, be selective. The healing of the relationship that leads to the healing of the life is always initiated by God who extends his grace to every one of us, not just a chosen few.[20] Wesleyans identify this as prevenient grace, and it restores to humanity the ability to be open or to remain closed to a relationship with God again.[21] This grace is understood as a gift that we either receive or reject, for "we have nothing which we have not received . . . the very first motion of good is from above, as well as the power which conducts it to that end."[22] Every aspect of our life is both touched by God's love that is freely given and transformed by God's love if we respond positively. This is only possible by faith in Christ. It is very important to note that because salvation is essentially seen in terms of love, which is a relational term, Wesley also views faith primarily in relational terms. Faith was "not barely a speculative, rational thing, a cold, lifeless assent, a train of ideas in the head; but also a disposition of the heart."[23] This

---

15. See Wesley, *Sermons*, 4:26, 37.

16. Wesley, *Sermons*, 4:356.

17. Wesley, *Sermons*, 4:355.

18. It may be objected that if God loves us so much, why does he allow this damaged creation, with all its pain and grief, to continue? For an accessible investigation of this topic, see Castelo, *Theological Theodicy*.

19. Wesley, *Sermons*, 3:544.

20. Wesley was an Arminian in his theology, and one of the distinguishing marks of this theological framework from Calvinism is the belief that God invites all to respond to his grace. This topic can be explored further in Collins, *Theology of John Wesley*.

21. Wesley, *Sermons*, 2:489. See also Wesley, *Sermons*, 3:545. On prevenient grace, see Crofford, *Streams of Mercy*; Rogers, "Concept of Prevenient Grace."

22. Wesley, *Sermons*, 3:203 (on prevenient grace, see 203n24).

23. Wesley, *Sermons*, 1:120.

disposition is to be understood as trust.[24] This trust arose in response to a person experiencing the love of God, and not because of their rational decision. As such, it is open to every human being to trust, even if the reasons for it cannot be articulated. This is seen in the response of newborn infants and toddlers to people who clearly love them and interact positively with them. He firmly believed that young children could know a rich and deep relationship with God.[25] As we saw in chapter 2, a person living with severe intellectual impairment does express trust in those with whom they co-exist in a loving and meaningful relationship. Trust, like love, can deepen and expand as a relationship is cultivated. We love a newborn baby before it is capable of any measurable response simply because it is a newborn infant. Parents, family members, and friends may have a deeper and richer love for this child than a stranger, but even a stranger can love a baby just because it is a baby. In an infinitely more profound way, God loves every human being simply because they are created in his image—no matter how damaged that image may be. What is more, he loves them even if they do not return his love or reject it. That is why almost every Wesleyan denomination believes that we all begin in grace, and only as we acquire the mental capacity to make reasoned moral judgements for ourselves, do we risk forfeiting the grace we have received by choosing to break the relationship with God. Therefore, all babies and young children begin in a grace-enabled positive relationship with God. This covers all those who, for whatever reason, are unable to make a moral decision for themselves because they lack the ability to do so. This inability may have been present from birth, the result of disease or an accident later in life.

Salvation (healing) involves a reciprocal relationship of love, but that does not mean it requires an equal depth of love by both parties. As 1 John 4:19 tells us, "We love because he first loved us." The love of God is infinite and unceasing in reaching out to every person and inviting them into a relationship with him. Human beings are finite creatures and our capacity for giving and receiving love is hampered by our brokenness, as is our capability (inclination) to further develop the relationship. As we have seen, we are all broken and therefore we all struggle to receive and give love to God and to one another; sometimes we are not even inclined to

---

24. See, for example, Wesley, *Sermons*, 1:121, 138–39, 405.

25. Wesley, *Letters* [Telford], 5:333. For another positive evaluation of the spiritual experience of children, see Wesley, *Journals and Diaries*, 22:328–29, 329–37; 23:355, 58; *Letters* [Telford], 7:96.

do so. The failure of any typically developing person to form and maintain a friendship with those living with intellectual impairment is simply one illustration of our ongoing brokenness. If healing depends on our unaided efforts, then it is doomed to fail, no matter the degree of our physical or intellectual health. The capacity for receiving and then for giving is not tied to our present abilities or intellect, because it is always capable of increase. Reflecting again on our relationship with newborn babies, they may begin life primarily as a receiver of love, with a limited capacity to return it. Over time, the potential is there for both the receptive and sharing capacity to increase. However, right from the earliest days, the baby can still bring enormous pleasure and joy to those who love him or her, long before they develop fluent speech or extensive mobility. A key factor in the relationship going forward is the future promise of enrichment and depth. That is why the timeline for thinking through our relationship with those who live with moderate or severe intellectually impaired is not the length of the human lifespan till the moment of death. The Christian perspective emphasizes that life continues post-resurrection in the new creation of God, whose love is infinite and who has created us capable of an unending increase in both our capacity for love and our inclination to share that love.

The Challenge of Bodily Impairment

Human life is bodily life and living in a world that is damaged means we cannot avoid experiencing physical and mental weakness, sickness, pain, deterioration and eventual death.[26] None of us is able to evade this reality,[27] and being a Christian does not prevent us from having to cope with the limitations this brings. Wesley reminds us that "the animal frame will affect more or less every power of the soul; seeing at present the soul can no more *love* than it can *think*, any otherwise than by the help of bodily organs."[28] There are "a thousand nameless defects either in conversation or behaviour. These are the infirmities which are found in the best of men in a larger or smaller proportion. And from these none can hope to be perfectly

---

26. Wesley, *Sermons*, 3:159.

27. For an excellent, but brief, examination of Wesley's understanding of infirmities and their relationship to sin, see Peckham, *Wesley's Understanding of Human Infirmities*.

28. Wesley, *Letters* [Telford], 5:4. See Wesley, *Doctrinal and Controversial Treatises II*, 13:528–46, for an extended treatment of the nature of the body and its relationship with our spiritual nature.

freed till the spirit returns to God that gave it."[29] He was convinced that God provided healing (salvation) through Christ so that the impact of our present impaired existence could be lessened through both spiritual and physical healing. As Hughes observes, "Christ as the Great Physician heals our woundedness and sin-diseased souls (the Latin term *salvus* means both healing and wholeness of mind/body and spirit) and makes us partakers of holiness, restoring the vitality of life that God intended for us."[30] However, while we can know a full healing in our relationship with God and neighbor, this does not guarantee physical healing in this life.[31] Wesley strongly believed that there was a close connection between physical, mental and spiritual health but he did not conflate physical and spiritual health or spiritualize physical symptoms.[32] The death/resurrection of Christ delivers us from our sinfulness and begins the healing of the damage that sin has inflicted but a complete healing from all illness, disease and bodily limitations awaits the day of resurrection. People living with moderate to severe intellectual impairment are certainly loved by God, and his Spirit is always at work within each one. However, there is no promise from God of a full healing in this present existence of anyone's intellectual and/or physical limitations. Modern medicine can bring healing for many diseases and illnesses, surgery can improve many physical limitations and therapy can help us cope with many conditions, and for all of this we must be deeply thankful. However, it cannot bring complete healing, and, from a purely human perspective, death remains the final victor.

> Affliction in all its forms confronts us with the brute limitations of our control over the course our lives take. Illness, disability, and suffering that are intermittent or short lived are more easily integrated into a general sense of competency and independence. By contrast, acute or chronic physical pain, sustained disability or weakness, or the toll of tragic loss and traumatic assault more starkly confront us with our vulnerability and often too with our need for the support and care of others.[33]

This reality means that for every person, sooner or later, we will need the support provided by others. "In a public, shared world that blithely

29. Wesley, *Sermons*, 2:103. See also Wesley, *Letters* [Telford], 5:284.
30. Hughes, "Holistic Way," 245.
31. Madden, *Cheap, Safe and Natural Medicine*, 34.
32. Madden, *Cheap, Safe and Natural Medicine*, 185.
33. Carse, "Vulnerability, Agency, and Human Flourishing," 37.

proceeds as if illness, death, and trauma do not exist, disease and affliction have no 'dignified' place; they are often silently or secretly endured, hidden from view, moved into the privatized, sequestered arenas of the home, the clinic, or lonely awareness."[34] As we have seen, this is the daily reality for so many living with moderate to severe intellectual impairment. People can live with many disadvantages in life if they know they are loved and can love others in return, even if the expression of this appears to be limited by their current bodily existence. From a Wesleyan perspective, we are all impacted by a range of physical and intellectual limitations and that has an influence on our ability to think, evaluate and judge. If we do not really understand a situation we are faced with, we will evaluate what we think we know and then often make an inadequate decision about what to do. As Wesley reminds us, a "mistake in judgment may occasion a mistake in practice, yea, naturally leads thereto."[35] One of the dangers of the dominant Western views of human personhood is that we are likely to judge someone living with severe intellectual impairment as less than a person, and then treat them accordingly. This may lead us to treat the person harshly or to ignore them altogether. However, relationships can survive unintentional blunders and failings arising from a limited understanding and faulty judgement if the person making them then genuinely seeks a different framework for their evaluation and then acts on it.

One of the struggles that many have who would classify themselves as "normal" is to actually see as a person the one who has moderate or (especially) severe intellectual impairment—particularly if that is also accompanied by physical and communication limitations. In a recent interview with Amy Illidge for the *Qweekend Magazine* of *The Courier Mail*, Amy recounts the experience of living with their son Jacob (aged thirteen) who has a range of impairments—epilepsy, intellectual impairment, autism, and mild cerebral palsy. He has the intellectual age of a five-year-old.

> Because of the way Jacob is, socially he struggles for connection. He's never been invited to a birthday party, he's never run a race. He's too good for special school but not good enough for mainstream school because he's not safe, so we describe him and kids like him as *the invisible kids*. A good day for him is when another kid at . . . school gives him a high five.[36]

---

34. Carse, "Vulnerability, Agency, and Human Flourishing," 38.
35. Wesley, *Sermons*, 2:406.
36. Watt, "Amy Illidge," 4 (emphasis mine).

The words "the invisible kids" sums up the problem faced here and now by parents and carers who have a child with moderate to severe intellectual impairment. Jacob is not literally invisible—it is just that other people do not see him as a person with whom they could have a friendship. Trevin Wax reminds us that what we pay attention to matters, and the fact that we pay someone or something attention impacts us more than we often realize. Based on the research in neuroscience undertaken by Iain McGilchrist, he notes that we pay different levels of attention to different objects. The attention we give to an object defines its value for us; it changes the way we see it and even impacts the way others see it as we talk about it[37] "Attention is a moral act: it creates, brings aspects of things into being, but in doing so makes others recede. What a thing is depends on who is attending to it, and in what way. . . . Attention has consequences."[38] If people don't "see" Jacob because of his impairments (and the judgements they have made about that, intentional or not), then they won't pay him any attention. The failure to pay attention then reinforces the message that Jacob is not worth relating to—he is "invisible." On the other hand, if a person was to pay attention to Jacob and engage with him as a person, then he becomes for them what he has in fact been all along, and as they talk about him positively to others, they too will be more likely to engage with him on a personal basis.

This is illustrated by the sharp contrast between the way that Jesus saw the presence of young children being brought to him to be blessed and the reaction of his disciples (Matt 19:13–15; Mark 10:13–15; Luke 18:15–17). The disciples saw a distraction from the main event, but Jesus paid them attention (Luke makes it explicit that babies were brought to him) and said they modelled life in the kingdom of God. "What we attend to, and how we attend to it, changes it and changes us. Seeing is not just 'the most efficient mechanism for acquiring knowledge,' as scientists tend to see it. It is that, of course, but it is also, and before anything else, the main medium by which we enact our relationship with the world. It is an essentially empathic business."[39] This particular account is significant for those who live with moderate to severe intellectual impairment. Many would deny full personhood to someone because they lack a sufficient level of intellectual capacity (as defined by their judge). They are, therefore, not worthy of attention as persons, and can be safely ignored. This was the attitude of Jesus' disciples

---

37 Wax, "Being Attentive to Your Attention."
38. McGilchrist, *Master and His Emissary*, 133.
39. McGilchrist, *Master and His Emissary*, 167.

with infants and babies, who have limited intellectual capacity at that age. The approach of Jesus stands in marked contrast—the babies are fully worthy of his attention and he embraces them as members of the kingdom. If we are serious about being followers of Jesus, then we need to pay attention to those to whom he paid attention. It is this kind of attention, this kind of seeing, that Jacob so desperately needs, along with all the other "invisible kids" that we learned about in the interviews. This kind of attention enables a genuine empathy with the other that eradicates any kind of superiority and affirms that we are all impaired in various ways and to various degrees. This changes how we see and what we see and offers a genuine prospect of forming a friendship with the person. This is certainly a hope that we all can offer here and now to the person and to their family.

As we saw earlier, the dominant Western paradigms of personhood support a negative evaluation of those who suffer from moderate to severe intellectual impairment. Changing this perspective is not an easy task and it requires much more than simply providing new information. The attempts to reduce smoking rates in many Western countries by simply giving information about how bad tobacco is for our health produced little change until other aspects of the problem were addressed that sought to influence behavior much more directly. Randy Maddox reminds us that the early church understood that information on its own was not enough to change the character and behavior of new Christians from a non-Christian background. The "implicit worldview" of the new Christians had to change. This required information, but it also required lived experience in the community to result in truly transformed character and relationships.[40] Christians who fail to allow their understanding to be "interrogated by disability"[41] are inevitably going to perpetuate the inhospitable, marginalizing, and dehumanizing approach that appears so prevalent in our culture. "Christian theology claims that dignity is inherent in every person, not because of our 'natural' rights or strivings; dignity is bestowed in the incalculable plenitude of God's generosity creating us in God's image."[42] That means we are to love every person as our neighbor, no matter their capacities or

---

40. Maddox, "John Wesley," 123.

41. This is a term and an approach used by Yong, *Theology and Down Syndrome*. He brings every major aspect of systematic theology into discussion with the emerging field of disability studies.

42. Hudson, "God's Faithfulness and Dementia," 55. See also Taylor, "Health Care and a Theological Anthropology," 227; Wyatt, "Quality of Life," 4; Kinghorn, "I Am Still with You," 98.

capabilities. In Western cultures particularly, we need to be reminded that love is not just an emotion, but it involves attitudes, actions, and intentions. The content of this love is defined by God's nature and activities, particularly as they are revealed to us in the person and work of Jesus Christ. If we have experienced this divine love through a relationship with Christ, then that love must flow into every other relationship we have: "Loving another with integrity means you cannot do, say or think things that would damage or diminish the other and still claim to truly love."[43] There is nothing automatic about establishing and maintaining relationships with those who would otherwise be overlooked and neglected. If we are to be part of the answer to the loneliness and isolation of those living with moderate to severe intellectual impairment, we are the ones who need to change and actively provide for their physical, spiritual, and relational needs.[44]

We not only need to provide information about a different paradigm for understanding personhood, we also need to provide opportunities and encouragement for a practical engagement with people living with moderate to severe intellectual impairment. Our new knowledge must lead to new practices, new relationships, new friendships. If it does not, then the new knowledge remains purely theoretical and of almost no real value. This is one of the main reasons why Wesley emphasized the importance of the means of grace as an essential part of our Christian experience. These are outward signs, words, or actions that God uses as channels of his transformative grace.[45] They enable us to nourish our relationship with God and with the neighbor. Wesley refers to "works of piety" (directed toward God) and "works of mercy" (directed toward the neighbor) and stressed the importance of the latter as acts of love focused on service. They were not simply an act of the will, but a grace-enabled response to the grace that we have received from God in the first place. As we shall see below, becoming involved in the lives of people that many seemingly prefer to avoid is not likely to survive the initial encounter unless there is a degree of intentionality and commitment involved. Wesley understood that sometimes you simply must do something because it is the right thing to do before it becomes a pleasure for its own sake. It is very easy to say we love someone in the abstract but the real test happens when we meet face-to-face, and

---

43. McEwan, *Life of God in the Soul*, 4.

44. Wesley, *Methodist Societies*, 9:72. See also Wesley, *Minutes of the Conference*, 10:211.

45. Wesley, *Sermons*, 1:376–97. See also Knight, *Presence of God*.

have to deal with our prejudices and dislikes. "There will be many occasions when we don't 'feel' like helping another, or when we don't emotionally connect with a person, but we are still to feed the hungry, give water to the thirsty, clothe the naked, visit the sick and imprisoned for love's sake alone."[46] The Parable of the Good Samaritan (Luke 10:25–37) demonstrates how we are to love our neighbor. The Samaritan is the one who bandages the man's wounds, pouring on oil and wine as a means of keeping the wound clean, picks the man up and places him on his own donkey, walks alongside him until they reach some nearby accommodation, takes physical care of him, makes a payment to cover initial costs, ensures that the man will be well looked after by the inn keeper, then promises to return again soon and cover any extra costs that may well accrue while the man is returning to full health. This parable offers a practical description of what it means to love rightly—it is not just a commitment to love only those who love us, nor just to say you love others. Christ-like love will involve the engagement of our body, our mind and even our money to ensure the well-being of others. It is a love that reminds us of the disinterested gifting of all of oneself for another's benefit.

To establish and then maintain any friendship presents challenges, and we are being less than honest if we do not admit that from the beginning. Every human relationship has times of struggle and it is not just an issue when engaging with people who live with moderate to severe intellectual impairment. Being involved in anyone's life for any length of time (including the happily married) brings challenges and it is very easy to walk away when it becomes more than we are initially prepared to handle (as our divorce rates clearly indicate). This is especially true if we view love primarily in emotional terms. Wesley was very conscious of this type of difficulty and admitted that it can be hard for anyone to persevere in any challenging relationship unless God's love overpowers our fears and pain.[47] It is significant that he recognizes how authentic Christian love makes the person vulnerable to the words and actions of the neighbor and this can easily bring hurt and distress. The response can then so easily be withdrawal. If we are to get beyond our discomfort, it requires a personal decision to not only begin, but also to maintain the relationship. This is where Wesley's understanding of the command of Jesus to take up our cross (Matt 10:38; 16:24; Mark 8:34; Luke 9:23) is very helpful. Wesley said we "bear our cross" when, without

---

46. McEwan, *Life of God in the Soul*, 160–61.
47. Wesley, *Sermons*, 2:314.

our personal choice, we lovingly endure whatever happens to us. The negative experience is not tied directly to any intentional decision that we made. For example, a casual conversation with a friend might lead unexpectedly to painful disagreement over a planned course of action. On the other hand, we "take up our cross" when we voluntarily suffer what is in our power to avoid. That is, knowing in advance that the friend sharply disagrees over a planned course of action, I still choose to meet with him when I could have easily avoided it. In the first case, I can legitimately feel upset because it was an unexpected difficulty; in the second case I cannot because I chose to meet knowing in advance it was going to be painful. In taking up the cross we are intentionally choosing to endure, if necessary, suffering and pain for the sake of the neighbor. This is not always demanded of us, and very often it will cost us no more than our time, energy or convenience.

A very practical illustration of this is given in Wesley's extensive correspondence with Miss J. C. March, who was a wealthy, educated lady.[48] She wanted her spiritual life to flourish and to know the fullness of God's love in her heart. Wesley told her that this would not happen automatically, and she must be involved in forming real relationships with, in her case, the poor and sick in their hovels if her life with God and neighbor was to flourish. This was not something that she wanted to do, given her lifestyle and status. She was happy to pay others to do it and to give money to help, but she did not want personal involvement. Wesley tells her that she must put off the gentlewoman, "take up your cross," and follow the example of Jesus.[49] The wisdom Wesley offered in the eighteenth century is no less pertinent today, and it is applicable to relationships in the family, workplace, and social settings. We certainly can make contact by phone, internet, email, text, and video today and sometimes these are easier to manage than face-to-face meetings. No matter how wonderful our technology is, it cannot substitute for physical presence. You cannot fully love another from a distance—the incarnation of Christ is the most profound evidence for that.

> Wesley powerfully reminds us that love is not simply a warm, fuzzy, feeling and there are times when anything but positive emotions will accompany our service for Christ. While feelings are an essential part of our humanity, they are not to be the master of our lives—that is to be Christ alone. A genuine love for Christ and the neighbour means that we decide whether we will or will not

---

48. For a fuller account, see McEwan, *Life of God in the Soul*, 141–52.
49. Wesley, *Letters* [Telford], 6:153.

engage in the service God has for us and our emotions may or may not be in harmony with that decision.[50]

Thus, the importance of intentionally seeking to form, develop, and maintain genuine friendships.

---

50. McEwan, *Life of God in the Soul*, 151.

5

The Family and Friendships

IN THE INTRODUCTORY PAGES of our book we referred to the story of Max and his family. Late one night, at the end of a heartbreaking day, Max's dad uttered the words that have reverberated deeply and regularly in our writing process: "Where is the hope for Max? Where is the hope for our family?" Many of the families Jim interviewed feel isolated, alone, and deeply concerned about the future of their much-loved son or daughter. The sheer workload that parents (and often siblings) face in caring for a child living with moderate to severe intellectual impairment is staggering. From the moment of initial diagnosis, families are involved in an unending round of appointments with a range of hospital departments while trying to hold all the pieces of the medical puzzle together so that they can understand the picture as a whole. As their child gets older, they must then add all the requirements of the special needs system, along with the various therapies and activities they need to be a part of. Many of these appointments are in different areas of the city and, especially for parents in rural areas, they involve a lot of travel. For both medical and therapy interventions, there is a great deal of paperwork to be kept and regularly updated. Little wonder that the daily, weekly, and monthly calendar fills so quickly with these things that are essential, leaving little room for coping with the needs of other children, their partner, or their friends. For some children living with multiple and severe impairments, there is a constant worry about their survival through the night, listening for the machinery that monitors their condition, rising to administer medications or perform a needed therapy. All of this produces an enormous mental, physical, and emotional load for the parents to carry. It leaves little time to tend to their own needs, especially when a burden of guilt so often accompanies their efforts.[1] Apart from the demands of medical and therapy appointments, the routines of daily living are often overwhelming:

> The amount of extra physical care and effort that goes into the day-to-day is huge: Dressing children who perhaps are unable to sit, stand or help to facilitate the dressing process; Lifting—there is a lot of lifting of growing children and moving from room to room, in and out of the house, then out into the world. Just a trip to the local supermarket can be a huge process; Organising—the preparation involved, there are not many plan B's; Feeding—for some, safe feeding with pureed food because of the risk of aspirating and the time involved with tube or PEG fed meals; Communication—deciphering your child's needs when there is no or little verbal speech can be very difficult. Again, a complex amount of time and space is taken up by parents wondering, did they provide the right thing at the right time? Was their child hungry or did they have an itch on their back they couldn't reach? Did they need to go to the toilet or did they want to wear the other shoes? Were they feeling unwell or were they just being extra quiet. The guessing game alone can take up so much mental space.[2]

The lives of parents and siblings who love and care for someone living with intellectual impairment is extraordinarily challenging. This book is a response to that reality. And the key response is tied up in just one word—friendship!

Genuine friendships with people living with an intellectual impairment and their families emerge from a variety of circumstances. Very often people are already friends and then someone from within that network gives birth to a child with an impairment, or a family member acquires an impairment because of an accident, disease, or some type of degenerative condition. Sometimes a new friendship emerges with a family through their engagement with a professional service such as special education, support services provided by health professionals, post-school service provision or through long-term housing for adults. At other times friendships can emerge from a chance meeting in a local park, shopping center or while walking through the neighborhood. Regardless of how these friendships begin, it is their very existence and their ongoing flourishing that matters most to people living with an intellectual impairment and their families.

1. Roberts-Mazzeo, "Hidden Workload."
2. Roberts-Mazzeo, "Hidden Workload."

In this chapter we are specifically addressing friendship with the families. Such friendships are important in their own right, but they also provide the best pathway for a greater number of friendships to emerge with people living with an intellectual impairment (see chapter 6) and this was *the* priority of the families we interviewed.

Friendship with the Family

Kate Hurley reminds us that the impact of having a family member living with an intellectual impairment is enormous, ongoing and impacts every area of family life. Although the family is hurting and under stress, it is important to remember that the people who have a son or a daughter living with an impairment were not always in this position and did not always understand its full impact either. Apart from the parents and siblings, there will be lots of people connected with the family who will be struggling to cope with this new situation for a range of reasons. The wider family, friends and casual contacts are often initially unsure about how to relate to the immediate family. While their motives are undoubtedly loving, the practical outworking may well be unhelpful, disappointing, or even hurtful. To move forward together will need patience and understanding by all concerned.[3] It is important for families dealing with the impact of having a child living with intellectual impairment to remember that other people will not necessarily understand the new situation. Families may need to take the initiative to highlight the needs that have now arisen. A level of mutual understanding is crucial to the formation and maintenance of friendships between parents/carers/family and other people. Hurley, who has a child with autism, has written about some of the things that will be important for people to understand as they engage with a family impacted by impairment:

> At the time of the diagnosis the family has been changed forever. Understand that siblings often have difficulty with the disability. Understand that families often deal with a hostile society, that waiting lists can be long and services hard to get. Understand that disability is expensive, that the information can be overwhelming and confusing, and that their friends sometimes leave. . . . Factor in the complications associated with disabilities and we can begin to understand that these families are under all kinds of pressures.

3. Hurley, *Take Heart*, 72.

> The divorce rate is much higher for couples who have a child with a disability. Parents also have an increased likelihood of experiencing mental illness such as depression and anxiety. . . . Comments or judgements on therapy decisions and other medical choices sometimes only increase their anxiety[4]

The impact on these families may cause them to respond to genuine offers of help in ways that others find hard to understand. Such responses are due to these pressures and the seemingly unending tiredness that living with a child who has an intellectual impairment often brings. In one of the interviews a mother acknowledged that a lack of friendship cannot always be attributed to others: "I think the support can be there but maybe there are times when you're just not ready to accept it. You get a bit 'burnt' from some of the experiences you have in the community or from people who are close to you. So sometimes you don't recognize or realize the friendships you could have because you are reeling from your last bad experience."[5] It is important to remember that there is no single template for forming and maintaining friendships with these families. Each situation is different and brings stresses to the families in different ways, requiring a range of thoughtful responses. As one older sibling noted, "If you have the possibility of pin-pointing exactly where the most significant stress occurs . . . then you can help relieve their stress more generally . . . when families are stressed up to the eyeballs then you only have to take a little bit of that stress away and they can generally cope with the rest."[6] In what follows we have drawn from the material provided through the interviews and the many years of experience Jim has personally had through his teaching career, as well as his own family experiences. In offering the following six principles, we acknowledge that while we believe they will prove helpful, there is no single template that will guarantee the emergence or maintenance of a meaningful friendship. We recognize that friendship is more of an art than a science, and the reasons why some people connect, and others do not, is often a mystery.

---

4. Hurley, *Take Heart*, 71–72.
5. Interview 15.
6. Interview 4.

THE FAMILY AND FRIENDSHIPS

1. The "Go to" Mindset

In healthy friendships it is normal for people to visit each other's homes, or to meet at a venue that one of them may particularly like. When all the people involved are fit and healthy, we give very little thought to questions of accessibility or suitability, since everyone can generally cope with the location and environment. It is only when one of the friends has a mobility issue or cannot readily cope with a certain situation that they give some thought to the location. For families who have a child living with moderate to severe intellectual impairment, this is a constant challenge. They often need a safe physical environment so that the person cannot harm themselves inadvertently. Sometimes it is a matter of physical access for a wheelchair, sometimes it requires a setting free from loud noises and bright lights. Some of these elements are obvious, but others are not and so are easily overlooked when seeking to build a friendship. It is important to remember that sometimes people came to Jesus where he was, and at other times he deliberately went to them. Many of the parables that he told, and the relationships he initiated demonstrate that God is a seeking God, who intentionally reaches out to those who are excluded from public areas or private homes because of illness, social status, occupation, gender or nationality. The whole point of the Incarnation was God coming to be with people where they were and as they were. God "goes to" because he longs to "be with." God comes to us because he loves and values us, desires to be with us, and longs to provide for us. This is true even in those times when we do not desire to be with him, or when we reject him. Yet, in and through rejection God continues to make the offer. All Christians are called, empowered, and enabled to be this same kind of friend, following God's example. Families coping with the impact of impairment need Christians to be that type of friend. This "go to" mindset is one of the single most significant gifts we can offer a person living with intellectual impairment and their family. It requires a willingness to go into someone's home and regularly visit them. But it is more than that. It is a metaphor to describe someone who consistently adjusts their own plans to meet the needs of a friend.

The need to be sensitive and responsive to the needs of a family coping with impairment is illustrated by one of the fathers Jim interviewed. This family have a child living with multiple and severe impairments, which includes seizures that emerge periodically, and which can then occur every few minutes for several days. Consequently, the family rarely goes out anywhere all together. On one occasion their son was going through a particularly healthy patch and over a period of a few weeks they went to a local park several times as a family. On each of these outings they happened to meet a local church minister who, on each occasion, invited them to his Saturday night fellowship in the local church hall. Because they were new to the district and many local families came along, he suggested it would be a good way to meet people. The program involved having a meal and playing some games together. While it was something they all would have liked to do, they explained that it would not be possible because the hall as described would not meet their son's needs. The family said they would very much appreciate it if he would come and visit in their home, as both the house and backyard were set up to meet the specific requirements of their child. This would enable all of them to spend time together socializing. Each time they met the minister in the following weeks they had the same conversation, but it never resulted in a home visit. The family has never been to the church hall, and no-one from the church has ever been to their home.[7] It was a lost opportunity to establish a much-needed friendship. The child could only be catered for safely and effectively within the setting of his own home and backyard. By providing for their son's needs appropriately within their own home, the parents would then be free to participate meaningfully in a social event. Since their son would be in his favorite environment, people would be able to see him at his best and could connect with him. It was important for the local church minister to be willing to go to the family home, for only in this way could he offer this potential friendship a chance to be established. Such an attitude is an essential ingredient in enabling people who have a child living with impairment the opportunity to connect with their local community. Sadly, this is not an isolated case, and in one of the interviews another father asked, in an obvious tone of disappointment, "Didn't the local church used to be good at visiting people in their own homes?"[8]

One Christian family shared how much they missed being part of their church community after the birth of their son who lives with an intellectual impairment. They could not attend their local church because they were unable to keep their son safe in that environment. Had the church been willing to make some minimal adjustments to its physical environment, then they would have all attended enthusiastically as a family. In fact, their son with an intellectual impairment was arguably the most eager

---

7. Interview 27.

8. Interview 1. A similar story was recounted in Interview 14.

to attend, "even if it just meant being able to color in a picture of Jesus while sitting within the building." His mum said that "He loves the look of church buildings. When we drive past a church he always calls out "Jesus" and it would be so good for us if we could all go to something as a family and if Oliver could be supported and still get spiritual input."[9] Other parents expressed a similar desire and one mum commented how much "We'd love to worship God with other Christians but going to church safely is an impossibility for us." They long for some Christians who are willing to come and worship with them in their home.[10] If needs like this are to be met, then people must be willing to connect with families in their homes and not simply at education facilities, medical and allied health clinics, local churches or other community venues.

2. Consistent Involvement

During our interviews, a parent expressed how grateful he was to the many people who have been so generous to his family. This included the support offered by the government, the health system, and the education system. "But there is actually something that we have wanted as a family even more than all of that generosity—it's a greater number of friends who live close enough to be involved. Friends for us and friends for our daughter."[11] This is echoed by most of the families that were interviewed—the need for long-term friendships that are genuine, consistent, and practical. A mother spoke in glowing terms about her lasting friendship with a retired woman that has emerged out of a community-run volunteer program. She noted the importance of having this friend come at the same time each week, and her willingness and ability to listen well while offering practical assistance around the home. "She has been that friend who has given us the extra pair of hands we've needed."[12] Another mother spoke of the decade-long friendship that has developed out of a paid service being offered by an allied health professional. One of the things this mother appreciates most is this woman's willingness to offer a non-judgmental listening ear, even during her own health difficulties: "She's consistent, she never judges you, she gives practical advice and she can always make

9. Interview 14.
10. Interview 11.
11. Interview 19.
12. Interview 6.

you feel better by telling a story about how others have gone through what you're going through now."[13] While meaningful connections can be made through paid services and volunteer initiatives, most instances of helpful relationships occur in other ways. For example, in some cases genuine friendships pre-date the discovery of an impairment and continue thereafter. There are instances where a friendship emerges with other families who also have a child living with impairment.

In one of the interviews we learned about two couples who were enjoying a very close friendship. While one of the couples was on honeymoon, their friends at home learned that their unborn baby had been identified as having some non-typical development in the womb. The honeymooning couple were immediately informed, and it soon became apparent that they had a choice to make: would they immediately return and become involved in the unfolding situation or would they wait till the holiday was over before visiting. They made the decision to return home immediately because "in committing to a family, you are saying that whatever pops up you are going to be there for them." They remained involved throughout the pregnancy, were at the hospital in those first precious days following Chloe's premature birth and have remained part of the family's life ever since:

> Over the years we've been willing and available to change Chloe's nappies, provide one on one supervision so she doesn't choke when she eats, share the travel to hospital appointments, help with shopping, or just sit and play with Chloe so her mum and dad can play with her sibling. When Chloe began walking, we would take a turn at following her around so she didn't run to the road or fall down the stairs. We have just wanted to be friends who were willing to provide that extra set of hands.[14]

Their desire is to remain involved for the long-term: "We know that it needs to be a realistic commitment but we want our friends to know we are definitely there for them, and that we are there because we want to be there. . . . We want our friendship to continue right through Chloe's life."[15] One mother particularly appreciates how long-term friends accept her whole family just for who they are and just as they are:

> They come here and they don't expect the house will be clean or real tidy. I don't have to feel guilty because I know they don't care what

13. Interview 15.
14. Interview 5.
15. Interview 5.

shape the house is in. They are worried about me and they've come to see me. There's also no barrier or nervousness for them around Oliver. They get the notion of disability and I don't have to pretend or worry about how Oli is perceived or how we are perceived as a family. I don't have to put on a front or a façade with them.[16]

This quality of relationship is a key outcome for families struggling with the many challenges they face and it is a product of both regular contact and reliable support.

3. The Art of Good Listening

Paul Browning, a world leader in the field of education, released a book in 2020 that outlines ten practices that are essential to building healthy relationships in the workforce. One of the practices has a particular application for forming a friendship with a family impacted by impairment. Browning writes: "Nothing is quite as reassuring or comforting as feeling that someone is properly listening to you. It is a gift of compassion and empathy when a person is totally present for us, fully engaged, giving us their undivided attention: earnestly seeking to understand who we truly are. This is not an easy thing to do."[17] He points out that there is "a healing power" that is brought to the relationship through the art of listening well while being fully present to another person.[18] We are conscious of the fact that people are not really listening to us and we do not like it. This is evident when they regularly check their watch or glance at their phone to see if any text messages have arrived. We notice by their body language that they have disconnected from our conversation and we hear in their mechanical, automated response to our words that they have not really heard what we have just said. "What they are conveying by their inattentiveness is that you don't matter to them . . . and that they don't really have time for you."[19]

For families struggling to cope with the impact of impairment, it is critical that we learn to listen well. This is a skill that can be improved through learning some simple steps and putting them into practice. Browning suggests we minimize distractions by turning our phone to silent and positioning ourselves to avoid glancing at a computer or

---

16. Interview 14.
17. Browning, *Principled*, 28.
18. Browning, *Principled*, 30.
19. Browning, *Principled*, 27.

television screen or other potential interruption. If we are meeting outside the family home, it is important to think about whether you are likely to be interrupted and distracted by others known to you. We should then make appropriate eye contact (unless this is culturally inappropriate) because "not looking at someone while they are speaking conveys a lack of interest."[20] We need to be mindful of our own body language—when we really seek to empathize with a person, we subconsciously mimic their body language.[21] The goal here is to really listen to the other person, allowing for silence to be a natural part of the conversation. We need to be conscious of the fact that filling the silence too quickly or interrupting with our own experiences is counterproductive:

> Nothing is more frustrating when you are trying to express how you feel than when a person who is meant to be listening to you constantly interrupts, jumping in to share their experience, or finish off your sentences. . . . Most people do not share deeply personal experiences and feelings with you because they want you to do something about them. They are sharing because they want someone to empathise with what they are thinking or feeling. They want to be believed. Poor listening doesn't bear that fruit. No connection occurs and, as a result, the speaker is left feeling undervalued, marginalised and powerless.[22]

The temptation to give advice needs to be firmly resisted unless it is specifically asked for. The unintended consequences of being too quick to offer a solution to their situation is that we make the conversation about us and not the other person. "Listening at its best is a selfless act. It is about the other person and not you. It is about entering their world and seeing it from their viewpoint."[23] This quality of listening will help to consolidate a friendship with parents/carers/families.

4. Practical Solutions to Practical Problems

John Swinton has suggested that the early church "sought to create communities within which the impact of evil and suffering could be absorbed, resisted and transformed as the people of God waited for Christ's return to

---

20. Browning, *Principled*, 35.
21. Browning, *Principled*, 35.
22. Browning, *Principled*, 27.
23. Browning, *Principled*, 37–38.

earth."[24] He argues that the modern Western church needs to respond to the existence of practical problems by discovering and implementing practical responses—or, as he terms them, "gestures of redemption."[25]

> God demonstrates power in gestures that appear foolish and pointless in the eyes of the world. . . . In the cross of Christ, we discover victory and redemption, even when all that we can see is death and suffering. In the cross of Christ, we see one man behaving strangely: forgiving his torturers, crying out to God in lament, handing over the welfare of his mother to his best friend. These strange gestures appear small and weak in the eyes of the world. And yet, it is precisely through these gestures that we discover the possibility of redemption, providential hope and the certainty that evil will not have the ultimate victory.[26]

Gestures of redemption bear powerful witness to the fact that "the way that things are is not the way they should be or indeed will be."[27] We may wonder how any of the realities experienced by people living with intellectual impairment and their families can genuinely be changed—what difference can "I" make? In a recent devotional article, Selina Stone reminds us about the difference two seemingly unimportant women made to the future of the people of Israel and their liberation from enslavement in Egypt. The heart of this event is told in Exod 1:15–17, after Pharaoh, the King of Egypt, orders that all male babies born to the Hebrew people are to be killed at birth. Two midwives (named in the text as Shiphrah and Puah) refuse to do that and one particular male baby, Moses, grows up to be the liberator of his people. As Stone points out, these women did not hold positions of power or influence in the Egyptian nation but shaped the future decisively by their loving action.[28]

One positive way that people can get involved in practical terms is to offer hope for parents who are no longer able to raise a child who is living with an impairment. Swinton suggests creating a culture whereby the responsibility for the child does not lie solely with the parents but with, in this case, the extended church community as a circle of friends. In some cases, people may sense a calling of God to accept the opportunity of

24. Swinton, *Raging with Compassion*, 69.
25. Swinton, *Raging with Compassion*, 70.
26. Swinton, *Raging with Compassion*, 73–74.
27. Swinton, *Raging with Compassion*, 74.
28. Stone, "Resisting the Powers."

welcoming and parenting this child in their own family. In many Western countries the fostering or adoption of a child living with an intellectual impairment is heavily stigmatized in the eyes of some people. Swinton argues that "if we had a culture in which adoption was an accepted and desirable norm, then things would look very different."[29] The creation of such a community offers an authentic, practical, and faithful Christian alternative to the current tendency within our culture to terminate life. The option of adoption provides an opportunity for people who live with an impairment to choose "a place where they are welcomed and a place where individuals and families can open up their lives in ways that embody the fact that 'it's good that you exist; it's good that you are in the world!'"[30] Before we dismiss this idea as either too idealistic or too radical, we might like to reflect on the fact that adoption is actually a key theological motif running through the Bible: "To be a Christian is to be adopted into the family of God; to become sons and daughters, not by birth but through the graceful movement of God through the Holy Spirit towards human beings."[31] Within this movement we discover that God affirms that "it is good that we exist; it is good that we are in the world!"[32]

Adoption/long-term fostering is a powerful gesture of how we can use our time, our energy, and our homes to help solve practical challenges facing families who have a child living with impairment. One of the interviews was with a family who had fostered a child living with intellectual impairment. The new family arrangement was working well, and the relationships were obviously mutual, with love and practical support flowing easily in both directions. The foster parents openly admitted their hope and desire to legally adopt their "son" if the system would permit them to do so. They affirmed him as an "absolute contributor" to the well-being of the whole family while bringing "great joy into our lives." For his part, the young man involved plainly loves the companionship of his "parents" that he has enjoyed for more than a decade. When asked how he prefers to think of them, he replied with sincerity "I just think of them as mum and dad."[33] The

---

29. Swinton, *Raging with Compassion*, 207. He himself has adopted four out of five of his own children, and he reminds people that adoption is not an act of charity but an act of "welcoming a greatly loved child into one's life, one's family, and one's world."

30. Swinton, *Raging with Compassion*, 207.

31. Swinton, *Raging with Compassion*, 207–8.

32. Swinton, *Raging with Compassion*, 208.

33. Reference withheld for privacy reasons.

situation involving this family is a wonderful example of Swinton's ideas around gestures of redemption.

Adoption/fostering is by no means the only important and helpful gesture that can form part of an overall practical response in this area. There is limitless potential for responses to challenging issues when three parties (the person living with the impairment, their family and a third party) willingly engage in a friendship that is genuinely loving, respectful, and reciprocal. The crucial thing from the outset is to understand that the first and foremost gesture of redemption is friendship between all the people involved. Without this type of friendship as a foundation, responses to the practical needs expressed by families will be no more than charitable actions, ministry opportunities, or professionally run and paid services. These, it must be acknowledged, are genuinely helpful but they do not, by their very nature, meet the most foundational requirement of friendship from which practical responses can most helpfully emerge. Friendship is a powerful pointer to the reality that the way things are now is not the way they will always be.

It was apparent from the interviews that families prefer practical responses to emerge from a friendship that has permitted them the opportunity to be genuinely heard. Even if the greatest need is someone to simply listen, there may well come a time when they ask for help, or when they would be happy for their friends to volunteer to help with a particular challenge they are facing. The most commonly expressed areas of need were: the prevalence of guilt, grief and loneliness, especially in the years immediately following diagnosis; a desire for their family as a whole to have opportunities to play with other families; relationship pressures; the hope for meaningful work opportunities for their child following high school; and the final and universal heartbreaking concern—what happens when they are no longer able to care for their child? The range of needs and their complexity means that answers are rarely simple and often cannot be provided by one person on their own or even by a small group of friends. There are times when helping the family connect with specialist help and providing support through the process will prove to be the best way forward. At other times, being able to offer help in some of the more specific challenges families face will be very welcome. Many of these are listed below, but there will also be times when we must find creative ways to respond to specific, localised circumstances. In what follows, there are some specific examples that the families interviewed found to be particularly helpful, as well as some suggestions that have emerged from our research in this area.

Offering Small-Scale, Voluntary Respite

Many of the couples interviewed pointed to the stress and tension in their own relationship because of coping with the challenges of having a child with an intellectual impairment. One of the dads commented, "I think it is true to say that our relationship experiences more pressure, more lows, than do couples who do not have a child with an impairment."[34] A mother mentioned, "There's a lot to deal with and sometimes it's hard as a couple not to take it out on each other."[35] In some of the interviews people indicated that the need is urgent because parents are struggling and sometimes at the point of being broken by the pressures of caring for their child. The pressure on relationships is clearly felt by other children in the family and one son commented,

> My parents have definitely changed over this past ten years since the birth of Alex. There has been a lot of pressure on their relationship because of Alex and trying to work out what is best for him. The pressure boils up and then comes out in different ways. I would like for them to have more social opportunities together. If there was some way for my parents to vent their stresses, to have a holiday together, to talk with someone either separately or together. I would like it if they had more social interaction with other parents, but not necessarily always parents of other children with disabilities. It would be good for them not to be labelled as "the parents of a disabled child" but just as Tim and Cathy, a couple who have children. They have very few others they can call on to look after Alex other than myself . . . if I am away then generally there is no respite for them. Parents of children with a disability are not machines—they can't just keep going under that sort of pressure.[36]

A very practical help here would be to provide respite care for their child on a regular and predictable basis. In some situations, families said that it would be most helpful if the respite care could occur in the home of their friend, thus enabling parents to rest in the comfort of their own home. In

---

34. Interview 1.
35. Interview 6.
36. Interview 4.

other situations, parents were very prepared to vacate their own home for part or all of the night and welcome friends to care for their child in the very environment that best suits the needs of their son or daughter. Whichever location and situation works best, the intention of this regular and small-scale voluntary respite is to provide parents and other siblings with some "space" to work on their relationships. One couple interviewed were already enjoying the benefits of this "gesture of redemption." They noted:

> It was so weird when we did go on that first night out together after not doing it for years. It was like we were on a date together. And we dated quite a few times in the next few months. And it took us quite a while not to talk about the kids the whole time. And I had discovered that perhaps we had lost a little something in our marriage that we had never wanted to lose. But we had kind of lost it in the busyness of the kids and in the busyness of Chloe's disability. And it was so enjoyable to rediscover it.[37]

Some pointed to their preference for a date night to occur regularly on a predictable day each month because having this kind of routine seemed to, for some, bring even greater value to the whole experience and to the ongoing success of their relationship. Importantly, even though the primary goal is to provide the parents with an opportunity to be together, friends can also choose to intentionally use these respite opportunities as a time to deepen their friendship with the young person living with the impairment. As we saw earlier, parents notice whether you are looking to more meaningfully connect with their child, and they are far more likely to relax and enjoy their night together when they know that you are looking to strengthen your relationship with the whole family.

Providing a Safe Place Where People Can Meet and Relax

Parents, and especially mothers, commonly blame themselves for their child's condition, resulting in both guilt and grief. One mother shared how "as mothers we typically operate in a guilt mode most of the time anyway but being the mother of a child with genetically inherited additional needs means that this is true ten-fold."[38] Many mothers feel like they don't fit in with the mid-week mothers' groups filled with typically developing

---

37. Interview 13.
38. Interview 6.

families, and they are often alone at home when the father is away at work. For some mothers, finding a safe space for their child to play while they have an opportunity to share their stories with other mothers who have a child living with an intellectual impairment has been so important. Several of those interviewed spoke very positively about a specific early intervention program run on the same day each week by a group of trained and paid staff in a local hall. This offered a single-gated, fully fenced, and equipped playground attached to the hall for the children to play in. For the first hour, everyone would play together and for the second hour, the (mostly) mums would withdraw to a debriefing session with a staff member and a paid psychologist. This allowed a parent to bond with other parents going through the same experiences, as well as having the professional support of the staff. Everyone had an opportunity to share with the group and with the trained staff. This resulted in a range of strategies being developed that could then be tried at home. Through the feedback process, one mother commented that "this was the single best supportive experience during those early years following diagnosis."[39] Another mother said, "I met so many parents in that group that I've continued to be in contact with through to this day fifteen years later. So many of us went through there together and all of us found it really helpful. We made lifelong connections."[40] For more than a decade this specific program has helped many parents through their unfair burdens of grief, guilt and loneliness. This is where friends can be supportive by looking out for such programs and recommending them to the family. They can also volunteer to help with transport or minding other children in the family to allow the parent and child to attend. These types of programs could also be sponsored by a local church in their facilities (if suitable) or in another community setting. Another family shared how their local cricket club runs a special session for children living with a range of impairments and their siblings each Friday afternoon of the cricket season. This weekly event occurs in a cricket ground that is fully fenced, allowing all the children to move freely and in safety. The children living with an impairment and their siblings are encouraged to be involved and everyone is helped by properly trained cricket coaches and an Occupational Therapist. While the children are enjoying their time together, the parents can socialize while

---

39. Interview 13.
40. Interview 15.

watching the game and at the conclusion of the afternoon the club provides a shared meal and free drinks for everyone.[41]

While these programs have proved enormously successful and beneficial over many years, gestures of redemption do not always need to be so grand. As we saw earlier, it can be very difficult for families to go to an event together. Frequently one of the parents will attend with some of the siblings, while the other parent remains behind at home or in the car with their much-cherished child who is living with the impairment. The reason for non-participation by all the family often relates to legitimate concerns for the safety of the person living with the impairment, or the logistical issues surrounding their presence at a particular venue or occasion. The effort and risks involved outweigh the potential rewards. Most families who were interviewed shared their stories of this common experience. One father recounted that in most social situations it is essential that he and his wife have one eye on their child and another on the conversation they are presently involved in. With a note of humor, he observed that this rarely makes for a good conversation. He suggested that they would welcome one of their friends joining their group for the specific purpose of ensuring that their daughter was being engaged in a meaningful way. By having a friend providing for their daughter's needs in this way, and knowing that she was enjoying herself, then he and his wife could relax and enjoy the company of other people. He referred to this as having respite within a social setting, while continuing to have the comfort of having their daughter safely and happily with them only a short distance away.[42]

Providing Opportunities for Employment

People living with an impairment and their families commonly express concern over the lack of meaningful work opportunities following the completion of high school. Employment can affirm a person's dignity, develop self-esteem, give a sense of belonging, and of contributing to the family and the community. Just a few hours each day, several times a week can make an enormous difference to the person living with the impairment and to the dynamics of their whole family. It brings a much-valued predictable shape to everyone's week. One useful idea we came across during the interview process was for an online shop that would allow people

41. Interview 14.
42. Interview 27.

living with disabilities to display, advertise and sell their own products. This concept originated with a few young people in a small country town in New South Wales who are themselves living with a disability. It was then developed further by a supportive community surrounding these young people. A local businessman quietly goes about employing people living with an impairment for a few hours each day several times a week. He is providing jobs for fifteen people who live with an impairment, in whatever form suits that person and their family.

Creating Welcoming Homes within a Local Community

One of the greatest fears of every parent who has a son or a daughter living with an impairment is what happens when they are gone? One possibility is that their child will be looked after by their siblings. Several parents interviewed made comments such as "his sibling was born to that role,"[43] or "his brother is aware of his responsibilities in that area,"[44] or "we would never deliberately put any pressure on the other kids, but clearly we hope they will take on the role of carer."[45] This brings comfort to the family and will work well for many. For others, this will not be possible, and we have come across many instances where ageing parents are continuing to care for their adult child simply because there appears to be few other options. To meet this need requires some creative thinking from local communities. Swinton's suggestion (mentioned earlier) of adoption/fostering into a loving family can work well in some situations. Another response developed by the Christian church has been the establishment of L'Arche homes worldwide.[46] L'Arche Australia describes itself as follows:

> L'Arche exists to change lives by caring for and making known the gifts and intrinsic value of people with intellectual disabilities. We believe that every person has a unique contribution to make to Australian society.

---

43. Interview 15.
44. Interview 10.
45. Interview 8.
46. L'Arche is an international federation of faith communities where people with and without an intellectual disability share life together. L'Arche, a French word for the Ark, seeks to create communities where people live a simple life of work, care, prayer, and celebration. See "L'Arche Story in Australia."

> In the communities of L'Arche in Australia people with and without an intellectual disability share life in a spirit of care, compassion and friendship. Through sharing daily life, with all its joys and struggles, opportunities for learning and celebration, mutuality grows and lives are transformed.[47]

In Australia, the best practice for community housing for people living with an impairment seems to be the provision of a home in a built-up area that is run by a non-government organization. This home is then staffed by social workers who support the residents as needed. In some Australian Christian communities, we see a growing number of families buying or renting houses within walking distance of each other in a local area. One such example is the "committed companies" of *Cornerstone Community Australia* where families "share life together and join with Jesus in growing faith, hope and love in their local neighbourhoods."[48] Jim has been speaking to a number of Christian parties about their interest in the formation of a hybrid version of the L'Arche community, the "committed companies" idea, and the secular idea of community homes within urban areas. The idea under discussion is that a group of Christian families would purchase or rent homes within walking distance of each other. At the heart of this "committed company" would be a community home for a small number of adults living with an impairment of one form or another. This home could be owned and staffed as a localized Christian not-for-profit venture. Friendship between people in the various homes is at the heart of this idea, which would then form the basis for the formation of friendships amongst the other residents of the local area. Ideally this would have denominational backing to assist in the accountability and sustainability of this venture and would maximize the chance of it being replicated in other locations around Australia. While still in its formative stages, the idea is one way that Christians can respond in creative and practical ways to the needs expressed by parents who are concerned about what will become of their ageing son or daughter once they are no longer able to take care of them.

As we have already noted, all these gestures will evolve best within the framework of genuine long-term friendships. It is vital that they do not become a "ministry" that we undertake at our convenience or when our name appears on a church roster. As one commentator has noted, "Too often I have seen people embark upon 'ministries of befriending' only to see them get

---

47. "Community Life."
48. For an example of this, see "Community That's Authentic."

bored and move on after a short period of time with a devastating effect on those who have been befriended."[49] It needs to be acknowledged that the five gestures of redemption we have highlighted (adoption, small-scale respite, the provision of safe places, the generating of employment opportunities, and the creation of welcoming homes) will at times be both inconspicuous and mundane. But, as is highlighted by the story of Shiphrah and Puah, their impact can be both significant and long-lasting.

5. Pitfalls to Be Avoided

Like everything in life, there are several pitfalls that we must avoid when seeking to establish a genuine friendship with the family. First, we must not become so involved with attempting to establish our relationship with the family that we fail to give significant attention to their child living with the impairment. If we objectify their child at the start of the relationship with the family (or at any later point) then it is unlikely that the friendship will thrive. Jim continues to be haunted by the words of one father during an interview conducted several years ago. With a deep sadness in his voice, he commented: "I would just like people to spend time with my daughter, to give her some attention, to talk with her.... Sometimes people even come into the room and don't even say 'hi' to Sofia. It's almost like she doesn't exist."[50]

Second, be aware that it can be very unhelpful if your offer of support is made conditional upon the family asking you for help. People prefer that you make the offer without their needing to ask. As one person said, "It can be hard to ask for help. You kind of feel like you have been doing that from the moment your child was born, maybe even before they were born if there was a diagnosis given in-utero. It can be hard to take help from others."[51] Sometimes parents don't want to ask because they know how much is involved in being with their child: "We recognize it's a really big thing to look after Oliver and so we don't ask for that reason as well. We wonder of course whether the person can cope with it, whether they understand him well enough to look after him properly."[52]

Third, be clear in your own mind that what you are offering is a genuine friendship and that it is totally free of any other agenda. This is

---

49. Swinton, *Building a Church for Strangers*, 31.
50. Interview 1.
51. Interview 13.
52. Interview 14.

particularly important for Christians to understand. Parents soon sense if the offer of friendship is tied to a local church ministry. While some don't necessarily object to that, they want it to be something more than just a program: "I'd be happy to make some social connections from the local church, so long as there's not too much pressure to funnel me in to something else, something 'religious' as it were . . . so long as there was friendship and socializing."[53] Agenda-less friendship is essential, particularly for people who do not identify as Christian. As one of the people interviewed said: "An invitation from someone from a local church would need to be really broad, it would just have to come as an invitation without strings attached, it would just have to be about a potential relationship for its own sake and not so much about the church and its agenda."[54]

Finally, it is important to be reminded again of the danger of thinking that a single type of response will suit every circumstance. We need to remember that no two family situations are the same. There is a phrase common in special education circles that says, "If you have met one child with autism then you have met *one* child with autism." This is also true of families impacted by a child living with an impairment. It is critical that friends tailor their responses to the specific circumstances being experienced by that family.

6. Staying Involved

It is no mistake that this principle has been mentioned twice. Strong and meaningful friendships in these circumstances can take years to develop. One mother pointed out in our interviews that "it took twelve years before everyone (including our son) felt comfortable enough to go to their home and stay with them, without me. He is safe with them—he knows it and I know it, and over these twelve years our friends have grown together with me and my son."[55] Participating in a meaningful friendship with parents/carers/families will be achieved best when we make a long-term commitment. In the end, each friendship needs to cross a boundary—the boundary that marks the difference between interacting with the family because you feel like you have to and interacting with the family because you want to. When this happens, a friendship is formed in which all the people are

53. Interview 3.
54. Interview 2.
55. Interview 13.

both givers and receivers, where they are accepted for who they are, and are recognized for their intrinsic value and worth simply by virtue of their very God-given existence and identity. Crossing the line and staying there makes meaningful friendship a reality for a person living with an impairment and their family. This takes time. It will mean working through misunderstandings and arguments, apologizing when you have been wrong or have made a mistake, it will mean choosing to continue to be a friend when you feel as though you no longer have the ability, or the energy or even the desire to do so. Such a friendship involves many shared experiences, lots of laughter, and probably some tears. But once this relationship with the family ceases to be a ministry that you do and becomes a friendship that you enjoy, then it is at that point that you become a better friend. You become someone who relates in ways that are individualized, deeply meaningful and genuinely helpful. Crossing the line means participating in a friendship that will positively and unavoidably impact the lived experience of people living with impairment and their parents/carers/families.

A family that has been impacted by impairment needs more community, not less. It is important that the family be given the opportunity to be welcomed into a larger network of friendships. Christians need to live out of the reality of God's vast love, which has encompassed us all. God calls and empowers his people, both individually and corporately, to live in a single friendship circle large enough to encompass everyone in our community. God actively encourages us to create frameworks that provide the opportunity for all people to flourish in their relationships and where we enjoy providing for the needs of each other. People living with an impairment and their families have contributions they want to make to a circle of friends and this mutual contribution can best be achieved when we make the circle bigger. This type of long-term involvement also happens to be the best pathway for a stronger connection to develop with the family member living with impairment. In a myriad of subtle ways, the foundations for a stronger connection with a son or a daughter are being laid all through the period of consolidating your friendship with the family. Your motives, attitudes, and actions will have been observed and scrutinized from the beginning, and the foundation for a deeper connection with your new friend was being laid all the way along. Just as it is in most friendships, there comes a time when both parties recognize their desire to move an initial connection toward a stronger friendship. This is no different in the formation of a friendship between two people, not connected along family lines, who have vastly different intellectual capacities.

6

Friends for Life

As we think about what is involved in forming friendships with people living with moderate to severe intellectual impairment, it is important to remember what was said in chapter 4 concerning the current state of the whole human race. Every single person on the planet today is not physically, intellectually, emotionally, or spiritually what God intended them to be at the creation; we are all impaired in various ways and to various degrees. People who accept this perspective do not, however, always accept that they are impaired to the same degree as people living with obvious limitations. Alasdair MacIntyre notes that:

> When the ill, the injured and the otherwise disabled *are* presented in the pages of moral philosophy books, it is almost always exclusively as possible subjects of benevolence by moral agents who are themselves presented as though they were continuously rational, healthy and untroubled. So we are invited, when we do think of disability, to think of "the disabled" as "them," as other than "us," as a separate class, not as ourselves as we have been, sometimes are now and may well be in the future.[1]

They then try to measure, often in subconscious ways, the degrees of impairment displayed, and this frequently results in Person A considering themselves to be less impaired than Person B. The conclusion is then drawn that Person A is qualitatively better off than Person B and, perhaps unwittingly, Person B is then judged to be of less value and worth. As we saw in chapter 3, this mindset has a long history in Western culture, but that does not make it correct from a Christian perspective. The framework for these evaluations is always biased to the perceived strengths of

---

1. MacIntyre quoted in Hudson, "Dementia and Personhood," 135.

the one (person or culture) doing the assessment rather than being a universal objective standard. Thus, Person A or Culture A values intellectual and physical capacity over relational, emotional, or spiritual capacity and judges accordingly. This impacts how much we value forming friendships with those who are different. Wesleyans believe that God's grace enables a full restoration of our spiritual life with God in this life and for some a measure of healing physically, mentally, and emotionally, though a full restoration of these aspects of our life await the resurrection. In the meantime, we all make judgements about the quality of life that is normal and who therefore should be respected and accepted without question; those who fall outside this standard are then judged to be less worthy and are therefore often given less respect and acceptance.

Challenges to Forming a Friendship

In a culture that values very highly the intellect and personal autonomy, to demonstrate a lesser measure of reasoning and personal decision-making is to be devalued. Someone living with moderate to severe intellectual impairment has other qualities, but these are often either overlooked or discounted. This usually results in no real attempts being made to form a relationship, let alone a friendship, with people in these circumstances. Part of the problem, as we saw in chapter 4, arises from simply not paying attention to these individuals as persons, often out of ignorance rather than a deliberate devaluation. In an insightful passage, Henri Nouwen admitted that:

> Living close to Adam and the others brought me closer to my own vulnerabilities. While at first it seemed quite obvious who was handicapped and who was not, living together day in and day out made the boundaries less clear. Yes, Adam, Rosie and Michael couldn't walk, but I was running around as if life was one emergency after the other. Yes, John and Roy needed help in their daily tasks, but I, too, was constantly saying, "help me, help me." And when I had the courage to look deeper, to face my emotional neediness, my inability to pray, my impatience and restlessness, my many anxieties and fears, the word "handicap" started to have a whole new meaning. The fact that my handicaps were less visible than those of Adam and his housemates didn't make them less real.[2]

---

2. Nouwen, *Adam*, 77.

From our interviews it was readily apparent that friendships between people of significantly different intellects are rare outside of the immediate family circle. Some of the parents we interviewed implied that devaluation and friendlessness have a direct correlation. Other parents indicated their belief that people do not connect with their child because they consider it too hard and too inconvenient to do so. Social researchers have attempted to provide an explanation for this situation. Dan VanderPlaats asserts that the reason so little meaningful engagement occurs in this area relates to the attitudes held by typically developing people that prevent genuine friendships. Attitudes such as ignorance, deliberate apathy, pity, unhelpful theologies, and well-meaning condescension couched in charity. He believes that it is only once people get beyond these attitudes that a more meaningful relationship can become possible.[3] Are the parents mentioned above too harsh and/or overly sensitive? Are social researchers such as VanderPlaats accurate in their assessment? Opinions on these two questions vary widely, but that does not alter the fact that meaningful friendships between people of significantly different intellects are uncommon.

It does seem to be true that certain attitudes and approaches will make friendship less likely, as both VanderPlaats and the parents interviewed affirm. Too often we see those living with impairment as charitable cases and cannot imagine that a friendship could be mutually beneficial. Hans Reinders explains, "Seeing truthfully means understanding the reversal of the order of giving and receiving. To presume that one has something to offer to the disabled person, and to presume that this is the point of relating to that person, is to be forgetful of one's own primordial need for being healed."[4] Reinders is right to insist that our friendship is not first of all "a gift that we have to give" or "an act of compassion on my part" or something "that I am offering to someone."[5] Rather our beginning point must be the recognition that "there is nothing to give without the prior acknowledgment of what has been received."[6] We are friends with God because God has first chosen us, and his love enables us to become friends with other people. In a very important sense "friendship is something I receive before I can give."[7] It is in this mutual process of

---

3. VanderPlaats, "Maybe It's All in the Attitude."
4. Reinders, *Receiving the Gift of Friendship*, 345.
5. Reinders, *Receiving the Gift of Friendship*, 366.
6. Reinders, *Receiving the Gift of Friendship*, 366.
7. Reinders, *Receiving the Gift of Friendship*, 366.

receiving and offering friendship to each other that we attribute worth to one another—a measure that helps us to know the inestimable worth that God has always attributed to our being.[8]

There are a range of other reasons why such friendships are uncommon. One factor to consider is whether some well-meaning people hold themselves back from friendship with those living with an intellectual impairment because of their own genuine fears and concerns. This was highlighted during a recent conversation when a person, speaking on behalf of his family, offered insight into their low level of involvement with another family who are well known to them and whose daughter lives with an intellectual impairment:

> We would like to be more involved. But we are so scared about doing the wrong thing. We are scared about saying the wrong thing. We don't want to do anything that would hurt or harm Bianca. We don't want to offend Bianca's parents. We simply don't know what to say and we really don't how to interact properly. We do love the family. And we do love Bianca, we really do. We just don't know how to go about being involved. We really want someone to show us what to say and what to do and how to do it.[9]

This is a genuine concern and it is important for the families of people living with intellectual impairment to acknowledge this. There are good people out there who want to be involved in a more meaningful relationship but, by their own admission, they simply do not know what to say, how to act or what to do.

Another reason for the absence of meaningful friendships relates to where our culture tends to locate the fault for the lack of connection—too often it seems that the failure is regarded as lying with the person with the impairment. The common technique used by our culture to establish friendships between people of significantly different intellects is to address the perceived social deficits of the person living with the impairment. Those who are intellectually typical often appear to have focused their efforts on the development and delivery of social skills programs for the person with the perceived deficit. Perhaps inadvertently, the focus is put on the more vulnerable person in this equation and their need to change, grow or develop through the programs being delivered. This results in a hierarchy where it becomes the role of the "intellectually and socially superior" to educate those who

---

8. For further reading in this area, see Reynolds, *Vulnerable Communion*.
9. Interview 26.

are regarded as socially inept. The belief seems to be if those living with the impairment could attain the requisite level of social skills, then they would be able to participate in more meaningful social connections.[10]

In what follows we want to suggest that the greater responsibility for the development of the requisite social skills should lie with those who are developing typically. We are not arguing that it is unimportant for people who live with an intellectual impairment to participate in a social skills program. Nor are we arguing that they are incapable of learning, growing, and developing—in fact, we believe the opposite to be true. Rather, we are arguing that it is an injustice to place the greater burden for developing new friendships on the more vulnerable person, rather than on the typically developing person. If typically developing people can be encouraged to accept that responsibility, then genuine friendships between people of significantly different intellects are far more likely.

Steps to Forming a Friendship

Whatever the reasons for the discernible lack of friendships in this area, it is crucial for people to know and believe that such friendships are possible. Unless we genuinely believe this, we are much less likely to engage in ways that will help to bring about meaningful relationships. It is important to be familiar with instances where such friendships have occurred and during the interviews many such examples were apparent. Many parents affirmed the value of the friendship they have with their child that goes well beyond family care, as do numerous siblings who recounted the real joy of the friendship with their brother or sister. A number of those interviewed referred to the friendships that occur outside of their family circle. A notable example where this has occurred is that involving Professor Henri Nouwen who had been teaching in several of the world's most prestigious universities for twenty years. By his own admission, he had never been close to anyone living with a severe impairment, yet he volunteered to help create a home for four men living with severe impairments in the Daybreak community of L'Arche in Holland in 1986. One of these men was Adam, a man living with severe and multiple impairments. Nouwen recalls:

> I still remember those first days. Even with the support of other assistants, I was afraid walking into Adam's room and waking up

10. See Duggan, "Implications of 'Special' Church Services"; "Reflections on My Life"; "Theology of Disablement."

> this stranger. . . . I saw him as someone who was *very* different from me. . . . At first, I had to keep asking myself, . . . "What am I doing here? Who is this stranger who is demanding such a big chunk of my time each day?" Adam often looked at me or followed me with his eyes, but he did not speak or respond to anything I asked him. . . . Gradually, very gradually, things started to change. . . . I was slowly getting to know him. . . . We were together, growing in friendship, and I was glad to be there. Adam was no longer a stranger to me. . . . He began giving me himself to be . . . dressed, fed and walked from place to place. . . . He was becoming a friend and a trustworthy companion . . . explaining to me by his very presence what I should have known all along: that what I desire most in life—love, friendship, community, and a deep sense of belonging—I was finding with him. He began to educate me. . . . He could not talk with me about the movements of his heart or the heart of God. He could explain nothing to me in words. But his heart was there, totally alive, full of love that he could both give and receive.[11]

The experience described by Nouwen is not unique. A carer for a young man with multiple and severe impairments recently confided:

> I have known Jayden for five years. I have worked with him reasonably closely during those years. But I don't think I have ever really known him. We have never been particularly close. But over this past two months I have been required to spend a greater amount of time with him than ever before. There have been few if any distractions to our time together and we've done a lot of one on one activities with each other. Things such as exercise routines suggested by his parents and that have been modified to specifically suit his needs. Or laughing together as we watched one of his favorite television programs. He has even begun communicating in his own way with me. . . . I've come to see that we have really bonded over this time, that we have a much closer relationship than ever before. It is certainly a better relationship . . . and I'm really stoked by the development.[12]

Knowing that such friendships are possible and do exist is an important step toward believing that such friendships can also be ours. There is no template that guarantees a friendship, whatever the level of intellectual capacity we have. All friendships have a mystery about them because they are

---

11. Nouwen, *Adam*, 30–37.
12. Interview 26.

not the inevitable outcome of a scientific formula. Nevertheless, there are elements that seem to be common in most friendships and the following eight principles offer a way to reach out the hand of friendship to a person living with moderate to severe intellectual impairment and we believe that they will work for anyone desiring a deeper relationship. From our interviews we saw that many family members were already making good use of these principles to build a much closer relationship with their child or sibling. Some of the examples given below are from Jim's professional experience working in a highly specialized and skilled environment. We decided to include them in this chapter to demonstrate what is possible, even in the most challenging situations. Most people will not face this level of difficulty and should be encouraged by knowing how much can be achieved in the right environment, with the correct help and support.

1. Intentionally Choose to Make a Start

When Jim first began teaching in the field of Special Education, he had no training in the area and had little meaningful involvement with anyone living with impairment or their family. He had been trained to teach English and History at high school level and had been given a job at a local school for students with mild to moderate intellectual impairment. Jim remembers well that first morning just before the clock struck 9 a.m. to begin his first ever school day in this new environment. He was frightened. Numbers had increased in the school and he was in a classroom that had been formed over the summer break by reclaiming a storage area. There were twelve desks for the students, a teacher's desk, and a mobile whiteboard with a few markers at the bottom of it. The walls were bare and there was nothing else in the room. Jim had no professional training in the field, very few applicable resources and little idea of what he was going to do when the students began walking through the door. He was very concerned about his ability to carry out the job. Noticing his obvious anxiety, his experienced Teacher Aide offered some wise words: "You just need to make a start Jim. I am here to help if you need it." Henri Nouwen did not think he could do it either when he was asked to help Adam:

> I simply didn't think I could do this. "What if he falls? How do I support him as he walks? What if I hurt him and he cannot even tell me? What if he has a seizure? . . . So many things can go wrong. . . . I have no training in this kind of thing!" Some of

these many objections I voiced; most of them I just thought. But the answer was clear, firm, and re-assuring: "You can do it." First of all, we will help you and give you plenty of time until you feel comfortable. When you feel ready you can do it all alone. . . . So, I began with fear and trembling.[13]

One of the most obvious things that neither Nouwen nor Jim initially realized was that a framework was already in place within which a new person could make a start. Firstly, there was a location for the friendship to emerge through the school or the residential home. Secondly, the location was safe for the person living with impairment and the new person because of its established practices. Thirdly, the key stakeholders (the person living with the impairment, the family, and the organization) had all given their permission for someone new to be involved. Fourthly, a generous time allowance was provided for new people to become good, independent practitioners. Finally, in both instances, there were plenty of other highly experienced and deeply committed people nearby, ready to respond to questions and to offer their help. These five points are not just true for specialist settings but apply equally to private and community locations. If we intentionally choose to initiate a friendship, it is helpful to be reminded that we also have a well-established framework from which to build. As we saw earlier, most friendships will develop from a prior connection with the family and that means we have a safe location (most likely the family home) with many other people (parents/carers/siblings) around who are heavily invested in ensuring their loved one's safety. The family, including their son or daughter living with the impairment, have given you their permission to be involved. They are usually prepared to give potential new friends the time needed to initiate and develop a new friendship and will normally be happy to remain available to answer any questions that might arise in the future.

2. Focus on Sharing Experiences

We indicated earlier in the book that strong emotional bonds between parents/carers and their loved one living with intellectual impairment were very often forged during frequent, intense, shared experiences. Of all the points we make in this chapter, it is this one that is the most important in forming a genuine friendship. Put bluntly, if we want to form and then deepen a friendship with a person living with intellectual impairment,

13. Nouwen, *Adam*, 41–42.

we will need to greatly increase the amount of times we share an experience with the person. These shared experiences need to be based around the other person's interests (not our own), and we may need to persist in sharing *their* interests or fulfilling *their* needs for a considerable period of time. Jim remembers how nervous he felt on that first morning in the new school. Not being certain about how to begin, he chose to fall back on an approach that works well in most new relationships—he made good eye contact, projected a friendly smile and started by making the relationship about the interests of the other person. In those first few weeks and months he tried to find at least one thing that really motivated each of the students in the class and made sure that he engaged with them around their specific area of interest. For example, one of the students was just about to turn seventeen and he usually communicated his preferences through gestures and a variety of sounds that Jim soon came to recognize. He had a huge smile when properly motivated and he could also make his requests known by writing in large block letters on a piece of paper, or sometimes on the back of his hand (with the requests always spelt correctly!). He loved street maps, train and bus timetables, car, and travel brochures. Making these the means to begin building a relationship, they progressively built their friendship centered on these areas of interest. Each week Jim would get this young man a new car or travel brochure, a new timetable, or a new street map. They would then spend time together reading and going over the detail of the latest car that had attracted his attention, or the latest location he was interested in visiting, or the most efficient way to get between two points in the city using his timetables and maps. Over time they built a strong friendship and often enjoyed a joke together.

At this same school, Jim discovered that one of his students (Tim) was particularly adept at memorizing large sections of dramatic writing, even though he could not read. The young man loved to act, and with the cooperation of the school and parent communities, a script was written, lines were memorized and then performed by Tim and his friends in front of a camera. From this young man's interest, a fully choreographed and costumed forty-five-minute film (*Butterflies and Moonbeams*) starring more than sixty students from the school was produced. The film was shown to over three hundred family and friends at the local cinema. Two years later, a sequel was filmed, once again starring Tim and his friends, and it was seen by over six hundred people at the local cinema. Shared experiences such as these are crucial to the formation and the development of lasting friendships. Almost twenty years later, Tim still greets Jim with a hug and a long extract from one of the films!

And that is how you make a start—some good eye contact, a friendly and genuine hello, and making your time together about the other person and their genuine interests. Over time you learn how to better communicate with each other, and that leads to spending even more time together as you discover a range of interests and activities that bring a mutually enjoyable, shared experience. Friendships may be structured around a wide range of indoor and outdoor pursuits. For some it can be around watching a favorite TV program, going to a movie, watching or playing a favorite sport, playing a board game, sharing a simple meal, walking in the park, swimming at the beach or local pool. The real-life documentary *Mission to Lars* provides a wonderful insight into how meaningful friendships can be developed by sharing in the specific interests of the person living with impairment.[14] This approach helped Jim's family forge a friendship with another family who also have a child living with intellectual impairment. Every time these two families meet, the various interests of the three children living with intellectual impairment are always indulged and the friendship between these two families continues to deepen. The evidence that this simple approach works can be found in the words of one of Jim and Mel's boys who regularly asks, "When are we going to Stephen and Bec's house?"

It is to be freely admitted that building a friendship is not always a simple or straightforward process. Many of the social rituals that help form and maintain a friendship are not applicable in every situation where intellectual impairment is present. Jim discovered this on his first morning at the new school when one of the students would not make any eye contact with him. He discovered from one of his new colleagues that the boy not only had an intellectual impairment but was deeply impacted by a secondary diagnosis of autism. This meant he was less likely to engage with some of the typical social norms. Over time, and through experimentation, Jim received a better response when his facial expressions very clearly reflected the thoughts and the feelings that he was trying to convey through his words. For example, using an exaggerated and prolonged smile when indicating with his words that he was happy to see this young man and the other students each morning. Gradually, the young man began to look in Jim's direction when he felt it would not be noticed, though he still would not hold a gaze. Jim took this as an encouragement that their connection

---

14. Spicer and Moore, *Mission to Lars*.

was developing, though he was never completely sure because the student did not seem particularly pleased nor animated by Jim's presence. This is why looking for something to provide a shared point of interest is very important, as it provides another way to connect meaningfully with a person. An obvious part of this student's well-established routine was just how organized and neat he was, both with his belongings and his appearance. Soon after Jim's arrival, the young man had retrieved a treasured set of highly complex jigsaw puzzles from last year's classroom and neatly stacked them on his desk. He would begin each day with the same puzzle, he would complete all puzzles during the day in the same order and would then disassemble and neatly stow them away right at the very end of the day just before going home. One of the puzzles was of Thomas the Tank Engine and this seemed to be his favorite. Jim organized to watch an episode of the TV show with the student and during the program the student became happier and more animated then he had been at any previous point during those first few weeks of school. Jim realized that each of the engines on the program have exaggerated facial expressions that are held for a relatively long period of time, and that was how he discovered the basis for a deeper connection as student and teacher. They worked their way through a whole range of curriculum areas over the course of the next two years, but each week they always made sure that their relationship grew by working together on jigsaw puzzles, an episode of *Thomas and Friends* and clear facial expressions that were held in place for slightly longer than the social norms of our culture would usually dictate.

Over the course of the last twenty years Jim has discovered that it is always best to use a consistent, predictable, highly individualized, and tailored approach for each student. This approach is particularly important given the range of complexities that are often being experienced by a person living with intellectual impairment as they go about their daily life. UK-based autism consultant Francine Brower paints a vivid picture of some of these complexities:

> Imagine living in a world where: the sound of a refrigerator humming five hundred metres away grates on your nerves; the smell of a person's perfume is like bleach and makes you want to vomit; you are oblivious to physical pain so that you are unaware of burning your hands when the tap is too hot; you would rather starve than eat some foods because their texture or smell is unbearable (like being forced to eat meat that has been rotting for three days); it is painful to feel the light touch of a hand; you can regularly feel

like you are dizzy and falling; you are not sure where your body ends and other objects begin; the frequency of light from a fluorescent tube is like a strobe light at a nightclub; you take what people say very literally; you have difficulty in understanding emotions, body language and facial expressions; you lack awareness of what is socially appropriate.[15]

Brower is not suggesting that each of these elements impacts every person, nor even a single person, all the time. However, it is important to know that most people living with an intellectual impairment have issues at some point in their day relating to sensory processing. It is very likely that their new friend is engaging and participating in our experience of the world while simultaneously doing battle with one or more of the issues raised by Brower. This tells us that people living with moderate to severe intellectual impairment are forging ahead in life with a high degree of resilience.

With the insights of Brower and other experts in mind, Jim has come to see the importance of being consistent, careful, and highly focused on the individual when forming and maintaining connections with those who are living with intellectual impairment. For some, a loud conversation or piece of music can be extremely painful to the ears, whereas loud and clear volumes are vital for others. Muted tones and calm (even blank) facial expressions are particularly important to some, whereas exaggerated facial expressions and excited tones seem better for others. For some it is always important to say what is meant, but for others there seems to be an obvious enjoyment in sarcastic humor. Varying smells can significantly impact the experience of one, whereas for others smell appears to have no discernible impact. For one person a gentle touch on the arm or the back brings reassurance, but others must never be touched because of their prior experiences or their sensory defensiveness. Some prefer lots of interaction through laughing and playing together, whereas others prefer to keep a lower, quieter profile by participating from a slight distance. It is important to recognize that some people respond quickly and others much more slowly to conversations. All these factors (and many others) can influence the success or otherwise of our relationship with a person living with an intellectual impairment. This is where advice from families and carers is so important and it will minimize the time spent trying to discover the unique needs and preferences of the person living with the

---

15. Brower, "Sensory Issues and Individuals."

impairment. We must not be afraid to ask for this advice, and then be consistent in putting it into practice.

Space prevents us from giving an example of how each of these aspects can impact a relationship in either positive or negative ways. But we do want to provide one example of an aspect that is particularly pertinent to the formation and maintenance of relationships: there is value in varying our wait times to allow sufficient opportunity for an individual to respond because of the specifics of their situation. One mother highlighted the importance of this aspect during her interview:

> Our son is non-verbal and his condition inhibits him from quickly responding to people when they engage with him. Sometimes people approach our son and say "hello" or ask for a "high five." However most often, when people do not get anything in return immediately, they simply move along without engaging. For those people who take the time to keep asking "Mate, how are you going? Are you right there?" and who wait for his response, well that means the world to us. Those people actually find that our son can and will respond to their questions and their requests, by making some beautiful eye contact or by offering a huge smile or by gradually lifting his hand for a "high five." . . . We are always so touched by those people who treat our son as someone who has feelings and thoughts. These are people who find out how best to communicate with our son and who then allow him the time to respond.[16]

All of this has relevance when two people of significantly different intellects make a start on deepening their initial connection. As we saw in chapter 4, part of the issue for typically developing people is their failure to actually "see" someone living with intellectual impairment as a complete person. Consequently, people are often far less willing to make the effort to act in ways that will help to initiate and maintain a potential friendship. We need to be able to see beyond the immediate (and sometimes obvious) negative impact of the impairment to the beauty of the person who is made in God's image. This beauty will only be seen if we are willing to allow an authentic loving approach that will enable us to discern the hidden depths behind the public appearance. This will always require a highly personalized approach that is appropriate for this potential new friend. It will involve a willingness to experiment with a range of approaches and an intentional flexibility to consider complications that may arise around the

---

16. Interview 6.

sensory processing issues identified by experts like Brower. It will be centered on discovering the best way to greet each different person in a way that is friendly and appropriate to that person's specific situation. We must then build from that point by finding and using this person's interests as the basis for playing and laughing together. As we proceed together, and as the relationship begins to grow, remember that we do not need to make all of these discoveries about our new friend at once, nor do we need to make these discoveries all on our own. In fact, the best place to get the type of individualized information that we will need to move ahead successfully, will be through our friendship and collaboration with the family. We will turn to the importance of collaboration in Principle Four, but before doing so it is crucial to note the importance of perseverance.

3. Just Keep at It

Developing friendships in this area may not prove to be easy or straight forward, but perseverance is critical if we are not to give up in the early stages. Jim remembers well his early experiences at a school in Brisbane that worked with students living with severe and multiple impairments—after just one week he seriously doubted both his capacity and his desire to fulfil the role. Each of the students in his class was blind, none were able to speak, and very few made deliberate movements. Inter-personal communication seemed impossible. The learning environment in that classroom required staff to be silent during the times when students were engaging with the individualized activities aimed at encouraging their engagement with the surroundings. All of this meant there were very few conversations in the room, and initially very few relational connections were made. Jim did not know what or how to do anything significant and could not see any possibility for the emergence of meaningful, lasting relationships. However, after two to three years of persevering with the situation, he was participating in the most wonderful relationships with both students and staff. Jim still considers the friendships that emerged in that education community to be some of the deepest, most enduring relationships of his life. It was only a change in his own family circumstances that led to him reluctantly leaving that school and that city. Seven years later, Jim still maintains that this school is possibly the most innovative and hope-filled education environment in Australia. This is clearly an extreme example, but the central point holds true in much less challenging situations. Even amongst typically developing people, a deep friendship sometimes only emerges after persevering with a less than satisfactory relationship initially.

In the beginning of his friendship with Adam, Henri Nouwen also held grave fears for his ability to develop and continue in the relationship—even asking himself why he had agreed to try. He saw Adam as someone who was very different from himself. Over the course of those first few weeks and months Nouwen continued to question his decision to be involved with Adam, and there were many times when he wanted to give up.[17] But Nouwen came to realize that thinking about the relationship only in terms of caring and helping contained an in-built condescension that was preventing him from engaging in a genuine friendship. People kept gently explaining to Nouwen that it was important to interact with a different attitude, that in the relationships within the community "we do not see ourselves as caregivers and patients, or as staff and clients."[18] It was vital that he arrive at a point where he knew at a deeply personal level that they were both givers and receivers in their relationship: "Gradually, very gradually, things started to change, and . . . my mind and heart were opening for a real meeting with this man."[19] Through perseverance over a sufficiently long period of time, Nouwen and Adam were drawn together as friends in a way that was enriching to both of them.

Persevering also enables new possibilities in the wider relationship between the person living with the impairment, their parents/carers/family, and the new friend. At the very beginning of the book we referred to the emerging friendship between Sam and a family friend from Scotland, John. During a beautiful Australian summer, the three parties involved made several trips to the beach. Usually Sam never went anywhere near the water, preferring to stay on the sand. This is where Sam and John spent most of their time together, with the parents trusting John to ensure Sam's safety while they supervised the remainder of their children in the water. On their last visit to the beach, Sam and John spent most of their time in the shallowest parts of the water talking together, playing, and laughing. A wonderful example of how a growing, trusting friendship can take all parties to new horizons. Journeying and growing together in a friendship like this will inevitably involve a level of risk. This account reminds us that collaboration is

---

17. Nouwen, *Adam*, 42–43.
18. Nouwen, *Adam*, 44.
19. Nouwen, *Adam*, 46.

vital in the management of risk, for the person living with the intellectual impairment, their family, and the friend.

4. Consult and Collaborate

When systems in the field of Special Education are working well, they are based on what some States in Australia term a Personalized Learning Support Plan (PLSP).[20] This plan focuses on the student's developmental needs, the supports and services required to address those needs and the assessment that will be used to track the student's progress. The PLSP is an umbrella term that includes a broad range of plans and it is unlikely that all the plans will be in place at the same time. The PLSP addresses a wide range of needs and can include: formal education goals, what programs and services will be used to address these; what is needed to prepare the student for life after school; which student behaviors are a risk to themselves or to others and how to deal with this; and what medications might be used in the event of a major medical incident that a student may be prone to. The preparation of the plan involves substantial consultation and collaboration with the student, their family and the professional staff involved.

We are not suggesting that the same level of training (or paperwork!) is necessary in a voluntary friendship, but a good friend will be strongly committed to consulting and collaborating with the person, family, and other carers. The importance of doing this was made clear by a father during our interviews. One of the things that he was very affirming about was that his son's school always took the time to consult both their son and the family to obtain their agreement before anything new was implemented. He felt strongly that these professional principles of collaboration should be used to undergird voluntary friendships with people living with intellectual impairment. He advised that those seeking to form a friendship should provide a support that is based on an individual's hopes and needs and on the desires and needs of individual families as they have been expressed. Trust needs to be built with all the family. It is crucial to involve the person with the impairment in these discussions. By doing all of this they would be basing their offer of friendship on the suggestions of the very people they are endeavoring to support.[21]

20. Bhargava, "Personalised Learning Support Plans."
21. Interview 18

A potential friendship can be undermined from the very beginning without the agreement and cooperation of *all* the parties involved for everything that you are doing. Even something as simple as failing to return to the family home on time because the person wanted to do something else first can create angst for the family who are expecting them back at an agreed hour. Especially in these days of mobile phones, it is easy to seek approval before any side trips are undertaken. Parents/carers/families are quite rightly protective of their loved one living with intellectual impairment. For a friendship to develop, and for risks to be managed, there needs to be significant cooperation between a team of people. Trust is hard to earn but very easy to lose and it is always best to move ahead with consultation and cooperation. That is why we need to be aware of the potential risks and find workable ways to mitigate them.

5. Familiarize Yourself with Issues of Safety and Well-Being

Persevering for long enough in a relationship with the whole family will enable a host of details to emerge relating to the safety and well-being of the family member who lives with an intellectual impairment. Before undertaking any type of independent outing with the person living with impairment, and before the parents will be willing to leave you with the responsibility of being at home alone with their son or daughter, it is vital that all parties are clear about the safety and well-being risks, as well as the mitigation measures that are required. As we saw above, if the person is sensitive to loud sounds or prone to sensory overload, what happens in these circumstances and how does the family manage the situation when this occurs? We need to be aware of the nature and general implications of this person's primary impairment, of any secondary impairments, and if there are any additional medical concerns (for example, epilepsy, anaphylaxis, diabetes, a heart condition, or anxiety). We need to know if these events are rare or frequent, and how the family manages them. We need to ask to be shown the mitigation procedures so that we are familiar with them before they are needed, and this may include knowing about emergency medications and how to administer them. If our new friend uses a wheelchair and/or hoists and lifts for mobility, are we fully aware of their proper operation? If we are using the family car for an outing, do we know how to properly secure the wheelchair in the car? Are there any circumstances under which our new friend becomes a flight risk? Does the family have a security system in the house to ensure that their loved one does not walk out of the house and onto the road? What is our new friend's level of pedestrian and road awareness? Are there any strategies the family use to meaningfully occupy their son or daughter when they are out and about at parks or when they are in the home? What are some favorite activities, music or movie genres, sports and/or other leisure and recreation activities? As we saw earlier, if we show an interest in discovering the person's interests, it helps to build the connection. In the event of an unexpected event happening on an outing, what alternative options would the family use to rectify the situation? For example, do they return to the car and put on some favorite music to help? Is there a preferred topic that everyone speaks about as a relaxation technique? Notice where the family goes for their recreation and use the locations your new friend is familiar with and enjoys. What types of food are particularly appreciated? Are there any foods that are strictly off limits? If our new friend uses a gastronomy button to eat and drink, do we know how to properly use the device for delivering these meals and fluids? Have we had a trial run under family supervision? What do the family do if the button pops out? These are just some of the considerations that a thoughtful and well-prepared friend needs to be aware of before embarking on an independent activity. The safety and well-being of our new friend is a priority.

There is one further point that needs to be emphasized because of its importance. In Australia and elsewhere there are well-documented cases of child sexual abuse. People living with an intellectual impairment are very vulnerable here and commonly face increased risks of being abused.[22] Sadly, a significant portion of this criminal behavior in the past can be linked to people who were acting as representatives of the Christian church. It needs to be emphasized that it is vital that we work to ensure the protection of our friend from abuse in this area. We need to be clear about what a transparent, trusting, and protective relationship looks like to the person living with the impairment and their family. For example, this will involve only ever going to places on independent outings that have been agreed to by everyone and then by ensuring we are on time when returning home. If there are any unexpected changes then make a phone call, explain what has happened and seek further permission for the altered plans. In many cases, we might need to apply for, and then provide the family with, a formal clearance from the appropriate authorities that we have never been accused, charged, or convicted

---

22. See, for example, Australian Government, "Brief Guide to the Final Report."

of an offence against children. In many jurisdictions, a clearance document issued by the police is required prior to a volunteer being permitted to interact with a person living with an intellectual impairment.

It is important to keep in mind that some parents/carers/families may never be comfortable with leaving their loved one alone with someone outside of the family or professional services. This may arise when the parents/carers/family believe that it must always be their full responsibility for the safety and well-being of their loved one. Being ready to accept without question their prerogative here is crucial and we must not be offended by their decision. If we demonstrate that we are unwilling to accept their wishes at this point by indicating that we are offended, or implying we know better, we risk losing the gains already made in the relationship. If the family is happy for us to be involved independently, then move ahead ensuring that you keep your friend's safety and well-being as your priority.

6. Remain Optimistic about Your Friend's Capacities

Optimistic assumptions can be helpful in the formation and maintenance of friendships. The school mentioned in Principle Three had a team of five staff working with a group of eight young adults in one classroom. As we said earlier, each of these students was legally blind, required a wheelchair for mobility, could not yet speak, and were incontinent. During one particular year there were twenty-six separate medical procedures each day for the students in the class. In that environment there was a strong culture amongst the staff of assuming that each student was able to hear and understand every single word that was said in their presence. Each member of the staff assumed that, given the right environment, communicative intent could be expressed in one way or another. All staff believed that if they were only perceptive enough, it was possible to participate in a meaningful two-way relationship with each of the students. Staff worked consistently with the student, their family, and their therapists to create environments that were exciting and challenging, fostering the possibility of independent and intentional progress. This required making the right types of highly individualized adjustments to the environment of the classroom to enable every student to grow towards their full potential. The motto was to bring the classroom to the student through a strong focus on ensuring the involvement, permission and support of the students and their parents/carers/family. These positive assumptions led to a hope-filled environment, with a framework that affirmed the dignity of each person. It was a place where learning and development was expected, and the formation of friendships encouraged. The important role of optimism is also revealed by the story of Canadian girl Carly Fleischmann. When she was a toddler she had been diagnosed and labelled with moderate to severe cognitive impairment and autism. When she reached the age of thirteen, having never used language, Carly began typing. Her parents did not even know that she could read or understand their speech:

> "We were stunned," her father said. "We realized inside was an articulate, intelligent, emotive person whom we had never met. Even professionals had labelled her as moderately to severely cognitively impaired." Among the first things she wrote was . . . "It is hard to be autistic because no one understands me. People assume I am dumb because I can't talk or I act differently. I think people get scared with things that look or seem different than them." When a father wrote to Carly to ask what his autistic child would want him to know, Carly wrote back, "I think he would want you to know that he knows more than you think he does."[23]

While the first example given is extreme, and one that is unlikely to be experienced for most people, both stories highlight the importance of optimism when faced with a challenging situation. It is vital that our optimism around a person's capacities always occurs within the framework of collaboration with everyone involved, but assuming the best will affirm and promote the dignity and potential of each person in the relationship. Over time, there will be some wonderfully surprising outcomes in your friendship.

7. Add Value Through Laughter, Communication, Employment, and Community

There are many things that add value to relationships and in this section, we want to mention four of them. The first is laughter. Through shared laughter we can deepen the connection and enhance the friendship, but we do need to be careful who or what is the focus of the joke. When we laugh *with* a person it is a powerful tool in forging a mutually closer bond. An example of this involves the student mentioned earlier who would regularly communicate with Jim by writing on the back of his hand. During one particular week, this student wrote the name of his favorite Sydney radio station (2UE)

23. Solomon, *Far from the Tree*, 242.

many times on the back of his hand and took great delight in revealing it to Jim whenever he got the chance. This was not Jim's preferred station and he saw the opportunity to have a bit of fun with the student by writing the name of his preferred station (2BL) on the back of his own hand before unexpectedly revealing it to the student when he next approached Jim's desk. It is important to keep in mind that Jim's preferred station was considered by some to be rather dull because of its focus on analyzing current events. Certainly, the student held this opinion because, upon seeing Jim's message, he hurriedly returned to his own desk, rubbed off 2UE from his hand, before replacing it with some new words. He then returned to Jim's desk to proudly reveal the phrase "2BL is dead," causing both to laugh long and hard, strengthening their relationship even further. But when our laughter *excludes* that person by leaving them as a bystander to the laughter of all the others around them, then it simply objectifies, isolates, and diminishes the person. It is far more demeaning still when that laughter is centered on the person living with the impairment or is at their expense.

The second is to be aware that people use a variety of ways to communicate, and words are just one of them. The school in Brisbane mentioned above had the benefit of a range of allied health professionals working with the staff and the students. One of the challenges faced by staff and students was how to develop and use appropriate communication strategies with students who were non-verbal, legally blind, and living with multiple and severe impairments. One brilliant speech pathologist spent a lot of time with the students and staff developing a technique that would enable a consistent yes/no response to emerge. A whole range of personal decisions can be taken when a person can communicate "yes" or "no" to the choices being offered to them. The technique that was developed and used collaboratively involved identifying a specific gesture (such as a smile) or specific movement (such as the raising of a hand) that was regularly and autonomously used by the student. The specific gesture or movement was then assigned as a "yes" response, and when the student chose not to use the gesture or movement it was assigned as a "no" response. Over a long period of time students began to develop their ability to express preferences by either using or not using the specific gesture or movement. This process affirmed the dignity of the individual by empowering each student to make their own choices. These choices were then respected, and in so doing every staff member indicated their belief that each student had something worthwhile to communicate.

Many of the students at the school were unable to eat independently, though some still ate orally with varying degrees of assistance. Some of the other students were not able to eat or drink orally and required a gastro button and tube for all their meals. The language and the practices used by the staff were vital in the process of ensuring the dignity of each person. Staff always had a meal "with" a student and never used the language of "feeding" a student. It is a small but vitally important gesture. To "feed" someone is to make them a non-participant, and frequently it becomes an act that de-personalizes and renders this person an inanimate object. When you have a meal "with" someone that is a different matter altogether. Eating together is an act of intimacy. In many of the classrooms, a dining table was placed in a prominent place in the center of the room for that very purpose. It was quite common to see a student sitting in a slightly tilted back position in their wheelchair at the dining table having their meal through their gastro button. They would be there with several other students, some would be receiving assistance to bring their spoon from their bowl to their mouth, while others would be taking their own smaller portion of a sandwich independently. And scattered throughout this gathering would be several of the staff eating away from their own lunch boxes. Staff and students were one group of people, eating and talking about the latest headline of the local paper found lying in the middle of the table.

Thirdly, it is important to realize that many people living with an intellectual impairment want to be meaningfully engaged in a job after they have finished their schooling. During the recent Australian documentary series involving adults living with cognitive impairment, participants were asked why they wanted a job.[24] There were a variety of interesting responses to this question, but they all affirmed the importance of self-worth and being valued as a member of the community. Building a good friendship involves helping others to achieve their goals. We can contribute to this desire by using our own creativity to help create meaningful employment opportunities, and by helping to connect prospective employers with our friend.

Finally, there is a well-known phrase that says, "it takes a village to raise a child." It reminds us that it takes a whole community to form the richest and most enduring friendships. It was very clear from our interviews that people living with impairment and their families want more community not less. Without adding any expectation or pressure, we ought to be inviting our new friends to become part of our broader friendship circle.

24. O'Clery, *Employable Me.*

Remember that this works both ways—we should be willing to enlarge our friendship group by entering our friend's community, too, opening many new opportunities for all concerned.

8. Regularly Check Your Attitude

One of the interesting aspects relating to the development of friendships between people of all intellectual abilities, is that they may begin as acts of well-meaning charity. During the interviews Jim spoke with a senior consultant in the field of Special Education. This highly experienced consultant has a personal connection in the field—she journeys through life with a much-loved son who lives with a moderate intellectual impairment. She made this important observation:

> There is a type of person who seeks out work in the disability field—either paid or voluntary—and I have come to call them the "bleeding heart" character. They could be a staff member, or they could be a volunteer supporter of the organization. Either way, they become involved with the child out of pity. They often seem to think, and even sometimes privately verbalize, "Oh, look at this poor kid!" Now, they're not deliberately trying to be condescending but their desire to work with the student emerges out of pity and sympathy. But I always say to them, "You are not going to last long here if you are going to engage with this person with a 'bleeding heart.' Because if that is how you look at things you are always going to find something wrong about the child. You are always going to find something to pity and something to be sad about." If a person only ever sees things through a lens of pity, then they will never see the child truly for who they are. And such people will find it difficult to have a lasting involvement with people in this area.[25]

An on-going attitude of pity will prevent someone from seeing another person for who they truly are. And until you come to see and appreciate a person for who they truly are, then a meaningful and lasting relationship cannot emerge. However, we need not despair if our relationship started this way. Henri Nouwen began his life in the community with a mixture of well-meaning charity and extreme reluctance. He had come to help Adam and others who were like Adam. Over time Nouwen came to

---

25. Interview 28.

see that thinking only in terms of caring and helping contained an in-built condescension that was preventing both Adam and he from engaging in a growing relationship as equals. Nouwen's attitude of well-meaning charity began slowly to change because of his daily involvement with Adam. It was important for Nouwen to arrive at a point in his relationship with Adam where he knew at a deeply personal level that the friendship was mutually beneficial, and that they were truly equals.

Arriving at this point is often difficult in Western culture because acknowledging the equality and intrinsic value of each person, regardless of their abilities, has many challenges. As we saw earlier in the book, the dominant models for engaging with impairment over the past hundred years or so have discouraged this attitude. For example, the medical model of disability[26] views it as a problem of the person, directly caused by genetics, disease, trauma or other health conditions, and this requires medical care to be delivered in the form of individual treatment by professionals. Management of the disability is aimed at a cure or an adjustment of the individual. It measures people against established norms for physical, mental, and sensory capacities and labels someone as disabled when they are considered consistently below these standards. The inherent tendency here is for a disabled person to be viewed in deficit terms. The charity model of impairment tends to look at people as those who need help because of their perceived inability to live an independent life. Well-meaning people, buttressed and motivated by this model, believe they need to look after, protect, and make decisions on behalf of, the person living with an impairment. Their intentions are good and often emerge from a genuine and heartfelt desire to help. Sadly, it also tends to set up a stronger/weaker dichotomy and this makes genuine friendship difficult. We have also seen that the depersonalization model of Peter Singer encourages people to reject the very notion that someone with a significant intellectual impairment is even human.

It is because of the ongoing prevalence of these various models that, in chapters 3 and 4, we have suggested a different framework to underpin our starting and finishing attitude. This is a model that recognizes the intrinsic value of each person because each is made in the image of God and loved by God. It is a model that points to the theological doctrines of the fall and salvation as a way of affirming that we are all impaired and we all need healing. This affirms that there is no "us and them" when it comes

---

26. This is the term that is most commonly used in the medical model.

to personhood, for all are equally loved and healed by God. We believe the model we have outlined can underpin deep connections between people of all intellectual abilities. As we come toward the end of this chapter, there is another account from one of the interviews that is worth recounting. It highlights how our attitude to apparently small details, does matter. One mother tells how she

> used to try to attend events with the extended family. I would let people know that we'd like to come to but would ask that William be allowed in the room first and then others after him. When noise gets brought into the room after him then it seems to be okay. But if it was the reverse, and William had to enter into a noisy room, then we just couldn't get him in and so we'd have to miss the party. People just don't understand how that minute detail can change everything. I've tried to get people to understand but people just don't realize that if that one little detail doesn't happen then "all hell" is going to break loose. I don't think I can blame people for not always understanding that. I'm not even sure how you can resolve that. Some of those really individualized minute details just don't seem to make sense to people and so they struggle to understand and follow through on that.[27]

It is so important to accept people for who they are, and just as they are. Small details do make a difference. It is crucial that we regularly reflect on our attitudes: are we still a person who is willing to adjust our attitude and our actions to aid the formation and maintenance of friendships with a person living with impairment and their parents/carers/family?

Who Do You See Now?

During one of our interviews a father noted that he never really had a deep connection with his son (who died prematurely in his thirties) until his later teenage years. It was at that point that he stopped wanting his son to be someone different:

> As a father you have all of these expectations about how you think and hope your son will develop. In his younger years my son and I actually had a very tense relationship because he wasn't the son that I was expecting or probably even that I was wanting. And it wasn't until he was about sixteen that I realized for the first time

27. Interview 15.

that I had to accept him for who he was, and exactly as he was. And it wasn't until I accepted that and started to take the time with him and started doing the things that he enjoyed, like going driving and doing ten-pin bowling, that our relationship really improved out of sight. And I started to really enjoy my time with my son. As I reflect back on that time I have come to realize that it was important for me to accept my son for the person that he was, and I needed to allow him just to be who he always was. And I noticed that my son's attitude to me started to change after that. The two of us really began to enjoy our time together. By the time he got to eighteen or nineteen I had fully accepted the fact that he was not going to be an adult person as I had wanted him to be. Instead he was going to be an older person who was still very young in his development, that he was still a child in many ways. At that point I had fully accepted him for who he was and just as he was. We continued doing the things he liked doing and our relationship continued to really grow and deepen. We really enjoyed our time together in the last fifteen or so years of his life. I was content and happy in his company, and he in mine.[28]

Some will "see" the person from the very beginning and parents in particular seem to more readily make comments such as "my son is my son, he is who he is, and I love him just the way that he is!"[29] For many the change in who they see takes time and most often seems to correlate with participating together regularly in activities that are much more than a verbal exchange. The building of a deep friendship requires this shared time and activity and we need to emphasize that this is not always easy at the beginning. One of the struggles in Western cultures is to come to terms with the fact that love is not merely a feeling. So often we have romanticized love and tied it to intense emotion through story, poetry, music, and film. The problem this so often presents is that when the intensity is absent, we can come to believe that love itself is also absent. We then conclude that we are no longer "in love" or that we are not loved by the other person. This issue was raised in chapter 4 when we looked at Wesley's understanding of "works of mercy" and its application in relationships. He understood people may find their feelings lagging well behind the act of being loving to a person. The feelings that we associate with love are rarely constant (nor are any of our other emotions) and vary under the pressures of daily living and personal well-being. As we have seen, this was true for Henry Nouwen, and it was equally true

28. Interview 27.
29. Interview 26.

for Jim while working at Narbethong. If we only act when we feel like it, then very little will ever be accomplished. When our feelings and our actions are in accord, it is certainly delightful, and it does make our relationship easier to maintain. However, Jesus has said that we are to love our neighbor whether the feelings are there or not. Every friendship goes through times where it is held together by commitment and putting into practice, by God's grace, the qualities of love outlined in 1 Cor 13. There will be the delightful times when feelings and actions coincide, and this will become much more frequent as the friendship deepens. That is why forming a strong friendship requires a deliberate choice to spend enough time together sharing in experiences that bring enjoyment and fulfilment to the person living with the intellectual impairment. This mindset will enable people to more easily participate in friendships that can make a world of difference to all involved. Such friendships can bring hope into the present experience of all and can point to the hope we can all have in the future.

7

Living in the Hope

WE HAVE SEEN IN this book that the greatest need of those who have family members living with moderate to severe intellectual impairment is for typically developing people to "see" a person with whom it is rich and rewarding to form a friendship. We looked at why, in Western cultures particularly, this is so often not the case because of the way we define personhood in terms of rationality, independence, and functionality. This framework was then contrasted with the Christian tradition that understands the human person as one who is made in God's image. From a Wesleyan perspective, this image was then defined primarily in terms of love and relationship, rather than the possession of several traits or the exercise of a range of functions. We then looked at the difference between what God intended and what has happened because of the wrong choice, the broken relationship and the consequent impact on the whole creation recounted in Genesis 3. We saw how God has acted in Jesus Christ to restore the relationship and heal this damage. In Christian belief, the relationships can be restored here and now, but the damage to bodies and minds, as well as the wider creation, awaits the day of resurrection. Based on the call of Christ to love one another just as he loves us, we then looked at what is involved in forming friendships with those who are living with an intellectual impairment, as well as with their families and carers. In this final chapter we want to turn our attention to the reality of the Christian hope of a day when, as Julian of Norwich said, "All shall be well, and all shall be well, and all manner of thing shall be well."[1] The quotation is not wishful thinking from Julian to us, but God speaking to Julian. She has argued with God for some thirteen chapters that all things cannot be well in the light of the suffering and pain

1. Julian of Norwich, *Revelations of Divine Love*.

that confronts us every day of our lives. God does not give her a detailed answer but offers her the assurance that God will through the mysterious action of divine love, along with his gracious power and wisdom, make everything well. God never explains to Julian "how" he will do this, but invites her to trust him and his promise to make make all things well. For people living with intellectual impairment, as well as for their families, that's the challenge—what are the grounds for trusting in a better future in this life, and not simply in the life to come.

Hope Here and Now

Ministry, programs, care, and a wide range of support are all needed, but as we have seen, none of these can replace personal friendships that go beyond the roles of client, parishioner, or participant. In the Introduction to the book we met Max and his family who were attending a barbeque with some friends. As we saw, the event was difficult for the parents. Even though they had friends present and involved with them right through the festivities, their son Max did not. At the close of that day, Max's dad was sharing some of his own struggles with Jim and in the course of the conversation asked, "Where is the hope for Max? Where is the hope for my family?" In other conversations with Jim he has shared the words of Psalm 27:13, "I remain confident of this: I will see the goodness of the LORD in the land of the living." He made it clear that unless the church can offer some kind of hope in the present, he is not interested in hope in the future. We need to be able to offer something concrete to this family (and many others like them), for whom waiting for some as-yet unrealized better tomorrow does not compensate for the harsh realities and the incessant needs of today.

To effectively provide an answer for Max's dad (and many others like him), we need to reflect on the difference between human optimism and biblical hope. Human optimism is based on projecting some aspect of our present abilities, capacities, resources, or relationships that have potential into a future where they can be actualized. Optimism is always based on what we see changing if certain things fall into place. Even with further advances in medicine (particularly neuroscience) and technology, more government legislation, education and financial support, it is hard to imagine a radically different future for those living with moderate to severe intellectual impairment and their families, though such advances may result in a more positive lived environment. It is this point that is so clearly identified by Max's dad. Biblical hope is different. It is not based on accurate projections about the future from our present, because the hoped-for future is not born out of the present. The future good that is the object of hope is something brand new, that comes from outside our situation. We have the clear promises of Jesus regarding the full healing that awaits us on the day of resurrection and all that will mean for our human existence.[2] Once more, as Max's dad says, this is all very good, but we need to survive today! If that is all we have, then it makes little difference to our present lived experience. The New Testament makes it clear that the ultimate future has broken into the present because of the death/resurrection of Jesus Christ and the gift of the Holy Spirit at Pentecost. The hoped-for future does not flow from our own resources—it is something brand new that breaks into our present. Because of Jesus's resurrection, the future benefits are already being made available to us now and the greatest of these have to do with our relationships—both with God and with each other. The power of the love of God shed abroad in our hearts by the Holy Spirit (Rom 5:8) is the source that enables us to be healed in our relationship with God, with the neighbor and with ourselves. The challenge for all of us is to allow this to profoundly shape our perspective on life, personhood, and relationships. This is where hope for the present can be offered to Max, his family and all who are in similar situations.

A recent article by Rosemarie Garland-Thomson offers three direct challenges to the hopelessness that so many experience. She suggests that three dominant perspectives in Western culture regarding people living with impairment need to change: the value structure of the social order, judgements on the quality of life, and the possible future of life.[3] In what follows, we draw on her article as well as our own reflections from a Christian perspective. Garland-Thomson challenges the dominant viewpoint that people are to be valued according to their abilities, their physical and intellectual capital, and their accomplishments. The typically developing person is granted greater status and value because they are regarded as being capable, rational, independent, and productive. Those living with intellectual impairment (and other associated health and mobility issues) are then downgraded and often seen as a burden on society. The charity model then graciously accepts the challenge of relieving or minimizing the burden but fails to accept the one living with intellectual impairment

---

2. For more on this, see the next section.
3. Garland-Thomson, "Conserving Disability."

as a person in their own right. This perspective is completely rejected by the hope we now have in Jesus Christ, where all are equally valued as persons simply because they are loved by God and are enfolded within the family of God. This is to be a present, lived reality. The second issue is the assumption about the quality of life. As we saw in chapter 4 our culture assumes that typically developing people have a higher quality of life than those living with intellectual impairment simply because of a judgement that is primarily based on capabilities, intellectual capacities, and perceived contributions. "The human variations we think of as disabilities are imagined to significantly reduce the quality of one's life due to functional limitations, bodily conditions and/or physiological/psychological impairments."[4] If the quality of human life is measured by independence, rationality and achievement (itself measured by a set of imposed cultural norms), then our Western categorizations might stand. In stark contrast to that, the biblical account of the death of Jesus Christ and the offer of the gift of the Spirit to every human being affirms that all are equally loved by God and embraced by that love within meaningful relationships. This is where the issue of quality must be determined, for God and the person are bound together in love and everyone is of infinite value in that relationship. As we saw in the previous chapter, the challenge for so many is to actually see the person living with an impairment, and not simply the impairment.[5] It is also in Christ that the future of the person (and every person) is guaranteed. The truth is that every typically developing person is always at risk of illness, accident, or decline, just as much as those living with impairment. Death is the reality for the whole race and none of us has a guarantee of when or under what circumstances that will happen. In a very powerful section of the article, Garland-Thomson says:

> The imagined open future of the normate [typically developing] and imagined closed future of the disabled arise from the cultural conviction that our bodies are tractable instruments of our individual and collective wills. A certain kind of body, modern acculturation tells us, will produce a certain kind of life. Our current eugenic reproductive initiatives rely on this fantasy of an open future that is understood to be secure in the ostensibly healthy and identifiably normate newborn that reproductive technologies and

4. Garland-Thomson, "Conserving Disability."

5. This is generally not a challenge for the parents we interviewed. For most, this was either their reality from birth onwards or was a point they arrived at through prolonged participation in shared experience.

treatments intend to produce. But all humans are, in fact, born significantly disabled: mobility impaired, cognitively disabled, and nonverbal, so that their normate status is always a *potentiality* more than an *actuality*.[6]

Here is where we can affirm that in Christ the full potential of every person will be actualized if they are open to a loving relationship with him (we explore this further below).

All three of these elements must be profoundly influenced and shaped by our life in Jesus Christ and the relationships with others that now makes possible. Everyone is valued just because they are created in God's image and deeply loved by him—who would dare to say to the Creator that they really do not value one of those for whom he died? But this needs to be put into practice, it must be lived out. People need to have frequent contact with others and these relationships must be stable.[7] This is why a genuine, voluntary friendship is so important because paid carers and support personnel may be changed frequently due to their case load or the requirement for them to maintain professional distance. It is not simply having a connection, but the quality of the connection that matters. The scientific evidence demonstrates that increased well-being and general health accompanies high-quality close relationships and feeling socially connected to the people in your life.[8] We are called to incarnate Christ and to serve/relate with sacrificial love, for only love prevents us from reducing people and relationships to a utilitarian value. Margaret Goodall reminds us that genuine relationships from the perspective of the new future promised in Christ can be genuinely transformative and enriching for both parties. As she says, it is "an imaginative participation" of the fullness of life in the new creation. This involves seeing and recognising people *now* for who they are actually *becoming* in Christ's love. In this way, we can arrive at the same point as most of the parents we interviewed—they no longer see their child's impairment even though they know of its reality. The importance of seeing, of paying attention, is underscored by a significant passage in a sermon from C. S. Lewis:

> It is a serious thing to live in a society of possible gods and goddesses, to remember that the dullest most uninteresting person you can talk to may one day be a creature which, if you saw it

---

6. Garland-Thomson, "Conserving Disability."
7. See Baumeister and Leary, "Need to Belong," 497.
8. Holt-Lunstad et al, "Advancing Social Connection," 517–30.

now, you would be strongly tempted to worship. . . . It is in the light of these overwhelming possibilities, it is with the awe and the circumspection proper to them, that we should conduct all of our dealings with one another, all friendships, all loves, all play, all politics. There are no ordinary people. You have never talked to a mere mortal. . . . And our charity must be a real and costly love, with deep feeling for the sins in spite of which we love the sinner—no mere tolerance, or indulgence which parodies love as flippancy parodies merriment. Next to the Blessed Sacrament itself, your neighbor is the holiest object presented to your senses. If he is your Christian neighbor, he is holy in almost the same way, for in him also Christ . . . is truly hidden.[9]

In the interviews we met people who were already living in this way and with this perspective. The type of relationship they were enjoying with their son or daughter cannot simply be explained by being family. A similar reality is seen in the relationship between Henri Nouwen and Adam, and with many others. For each of them this type of relationship is a present reality, a current lived experience of what the future promises in an even richer, more complete way.

Hope There and Then

In line with this, there is clearly an "already—not yet" tension in Wesley's understanding of Christ's work. He adamantly denied that physical or intellectual impairment originates from personal sin, nor is it God's judgement on personal sin.[10] Yet impairment is one of the many consequences of a creation now gone awry, for God never intended for the human race to experience damaged relationships and damaged bodies. We already experience a great deliverance from the power of sin but it is not yet a final deliverance, in which all things will be made new.[11] When Christ returns everyone will rise with their own body, though it will be changed in properties to fully reflect God's creational design. It is only then that our present corruptible body will be fully healed, becoming incorruptible and our mortal life will put on immortality (1 Cor 15:53).[12] Only at this point will the physical,

---

9. Lewis, *Weight of Glory*, 45–46.

10. This would not include the consequences of a personal choice to deliberately damage the body or the mind.

11. Wesley, *Sermons*, 2:365.

12. Wesley, *Sermons*, 1:358.

mental and emotional side of our human life be in total harmony with the spiritual side. The body will no longer be a hindrance to the full expression of love to God and neighbor. It is only after the day of resurrection and the renewal of all God's created order that we will be in an environment free from all destructive natural forces and weather patterns, with no more disasters, scarred environments, or violence.[13] There will be no more death, sin, sorrow, or pain, but "a deep, an ultimate, an uninterrupted union with God," a "constant communion," and a "continual enjoyment" of the Triune God "and of all creatures in him!" It is only then that we will be able to experience in full all the benefits of Christ's salvation personally, corporately and environmentally: "Hence will arise an unmixed state of holiness and happiness far superior to that which Adam [and Eve] enjoyed in paradise."[14] It is this vision of the goal of human existence that puts everything into perspective, especially for individuals and families who, because of living with an impairment and its consequences, often experience a great deal of personal pain and suffering during their earthly life.

As Wesley affirmed, though God's work of salvation in this present life is able to deliver us from the reign of sin in our hearts, it does not bring about a full healing of all the consequences of the fall for every person, let alone the devastation wrought on the rest of God's created order over the millennia. The final and full revelation of God's plan to renew all things in Christ awaits us in the life to come. In Rev 21 we read of God's intention to dwell with humanity in a gloriously renewed environment, a place where he will wipe away every tear from the eyes of those who have suffered in this lifetime, a place where there will be no more dying or mourning or crying or pain. The picture continues in Rev 22 which reveals that God will ensure all will once again have access to the Tree of Life that was mentioned in Gen 1–2. The imagery used is even more splendid than the original setting in the Garden of Eden and affirms that everything will be fully and easily accessible to all who dwell there. It will be a place where we not only enjoy meaningful, loving relationships but also significant, pleasurable, and fulfilling work too—just as God had always intended. These images provide us with strong picture of a God who longs for all to come and enjoy his hospitality, a God who wants to provide for everyone, no matter who they are or where they came from, a God who wants people to enjoy a flourishing relationship with him, with each other and with the rest of the creation.

13. Wesley, *Sermons*, 2:500–510.
14. Wesley, *Sermons*, 2:510.

This is anticipated in Luke 14:15–24 where we are told of God's desire for his house to be filled with guests for an unrivalled and eternal celebration. These guests are not only the typically developing people of the community, but also "the poor, the crippled, the blind and the lame" (v. 21). This repeats the comments Jesus had shared with a prominent religious leader at a banquet he was hosting and where Jesus was a guest (Luke 14:1–14, esp. v. 13). The emphasis is on everyone being invited, made welcome and hosted, including all those living with impairments.

The exact nature of the resurrection body and resurrection life is a matter of debate as neither Jesus nor the later New Testament writers gave much detail. It was an issue that confronted several Christians at Corinth, who wanted to know how the dead are raised and what was the nature of the resurrection body (1 Cor 15:35)? The latter question is particularly acute for those who have lived with a significant level of physical or intellectual impairment. Paul seeks to answer the question using reference points in our present creation to try and picture the reality of the new creation. He reminds them that the seed and the mature plant do not look alike, but the latter derives from the former (v. 37). The splendor of the resurrected body does not disparage the splendor of the earthly body. The earthly body (the seed) that is sown is perishable, sown in dishonor, in weakness, and is a natural body; the resurrected body (the plant) is raised imperishable, in glory, in power, and as a spiritual body (14:40–44). There is clearly a glorious transformation, but does this mean that those who lived here with physical or intellectual impairment will now be raised in a body and with a mind that does not have their previous limitations? There is no doubt that living with an impairment shapes self-understanding and identity, and so some believe that post resurrection the infirmity will remain, or else it is not truly "you" anymore. Nancy Eiesland, who was herself physically impaired, has rightly pointed out that "As long as disability is addressed in terms of the themes of sin—disability conflation, virtuous suffering, or charitable action, it will be seen primarily as a fate to be avoided, a tragedy explained, or a cause to be championed rather than an ordinary life to be lived."[15] In the light of the account of the resurrected Jesus inviting his disciples to touch the scars on his body (Luke 24:36–39), she affirmed that "in the resurrected Jesus Christ, they saw not the suffering servant for whom the last and most important word was tragedy and sin, but the disabled God who embodied both impaired hands and feet and pierced side and the

---

15. Eiesland, *Disabled God*, 75.

imago Dei."¹⁶ For Eiesland, the consequence of this is that "Resurrection is not about the negation or erasure of our disabled bodies in hopes of perfect images, untouched by physical disability."¹⁷ The implication is that if the physically impaired are raised "able-bodied," then they will no longer truly be themselves. The same framework is found when Frances Young writes about her son Arthur, who lived with an intellectual impairment:

> Arthur's limited experience, limited above all in ability to process the world external to himself, is a crucial element in who he is, in his real personhood. An ultimate destiny in which he was suddenly "perfected" (whatever that might mean) is inconceivable—for he would no longer be Arthur but some other person. His limited embodied self is what exists, and what will be must be in continuity with that. There will also be discontinuities—the promise of resurrection is the transcendence of our mortal "flesh and blood" state. So there's hope for transformation of this life's limitations and vulnerabilities, of someone like Arthur receiving greater gifts while truly remaining himself. Perhaps the transformation to be hoped for is less intellectual or physical advance and more the kind of thing anticipated in the present when the fruits of the Spirit are realized in relationships.¹⁸

Some physical impairments can be corrected by surgery and if this happens later in life, then we are still profoundly shaped by our earlier experiences. The later surgery corrects the impairment, but character and personality are still shaped by the past—the surgery does not correct "me." In a Christian framework, we are not just our early experiences and we do not cease to be "me" just because the impairment is corrected.

The key concerns here have to do with what makes us a person and what makes for our identity as a unique human being. Earlier in this book we examined the nature of personhood from a Wesleyan perspective and tied it primarily to relationship with God and then with neighbor and the rest of the creation. This was not to deny the reality of biology, or the traits that we may possess or the functions that we may carry out, but these are not at the heart of our personhood, nor are they the essence of humans being formed in the image of God. Neither an impaired body nor an impaired

16. Eiesland, *Disabled God*, 99.
17. Eiesland, *Disabled God*, 107.
18. Young, *God's Presence*, 107. For an extended discussion of this in relation to Down syndrome and with a similar conclusion, see Yong, *Theology and Down Syndrome*, 259–95.

mind impact the image of God in a person's life. That means that neither biology, traits nor functions are ultimately determinative of our personhood, and can therefore be impaired in various ways without impinging on the relationship initiated and sustained by God's love poured into our heart and the consequent connection that enables. It is this relationship that then forms our identity as a unique person, as we participate in the story of God, the stories of our neighbors, and the encounter with the rest of creation. Through these encounters we are shaped, and our maturing identity formed. The writings of Paul remind us that through faith in Jesus Christ, we are now "in Christ" and Christ is "in us" by the Holy Spirit, and our identity is further shaped by the participation. This is not an isolated, independent existence, but connects us interdependently with everyone else who has faith in Christ. Our identity is now being conformed (as Rom 8:29 assures us) to the very image of Christ—that is, his character, and not as a clone of his bodily image. In this new life, all our experiences and relationships are also being transformed through forgiveness, reconciliation, and renewal. It is only such a relational and dynamic understanding that offers genuine hope for those who died in infancy or early childhood, as well as for those who live with impairment—neither the immaturity nor the impairment define who that person is in Christ and what that will mean for their eternal future. At the resurrection it is their relationship with God and the rich tapestry of their life story that will guarantee their identity as the unique person known in this life.

That still leaves the question of their bodily state in the new creation. Many who write in the theology of disability field do so from their own lived experience and remind those who are "able-bodied" that they are not the measure of post-resurrection perfection. From a Wesleyan perspective, wholeness in this life is not defined physically by a perfection of skin, muscle, bone, or a symmetry of parts. Our culture's idea of beauty and physical perfection is not the measure used by God, no matter how able-bodied we imagine ourselves to be. As Wesley reminds us, the whole race is impaired, the whole race is flawed, the whole race is disfigured, the whole race is limited—not just those we label as "the disabled" or "the handicapped." Writers in the field of disability theology do well to remind us that some impairments are more obvious to us and we judge them by our own human standards, but it is God alone who sees the heart (1 Sam 16:7), which is where the real damage is done to our relationships with God, with each other, with ourselves, and with the rest of creation.

Neither the typically developed body or mind, nor the impaired body or mind are the measure of God's creational intention at the beginning of human history, nor of his re-creational goal post-resurrection. As Paul so powerfully reminds us in Rom 5:12–21 and 1 Cor 15:45, what it means to be truly human is displayed by Jesus Christ alone, and the goal of our resurrection is to be like Christ—and that we shall be (1 John 3:2). He is the only human being to have lived, died, and been resurrected (Rom 6:9–10; 1 Cor 15:20, 23); all those raised by Jesus in the Gospels being revived in the old creation to die again. The Gospel accounts make it clear that Jesus carried the scars of his crucifixion on his body—the nail marks on his hands and feet, as well as the spear-thrust in his side. It is important to note that post-resurrection, though he was marked by the damage, he did not demonstrate any impairment from the experience. If his resurrection body was simply a revivified pre-resurrection body (like that of Lazarus, Jairus's daughter, the widow of Nain's son), then he would never be able to walk the long road to Emmaus due to the damage sustained to his bones, tendons and nerves. The scars indicate his lived experience while in this present time, but they do not limit the possibilities of resurrection life afterwards. This would seem to affirm that we will all enter the new creation with the scars of our earthly journey, but not the actual impairments themselves. While this would not be accepted by all who write on the theology of disability, from a Wesleyan perspective the image of God is in the relationship, and it is this that forms the person and their identity.

It is certainly true that our experiences of life and relationships are impacted by a range of factors, including the presence of any significant impairment, but that need not define our future in Christ. If we reflect on the creation account in Gen 1–2, the description of the earth is that everything is good or very good, but not perfect, in the sense of being flawless and static. Life on earth from the beginning was dynamic and human beings had relationships to build, the earth to steward and populate, all of which involved work and development. Human beings had both the capacity to deal with the challenges and the capability to overcome them in partnership with God. God is the infinite Creator and we are finite creatures, and that would indicate that we have both a capacity for growth and the capability to do it by God's grace. The potential is limitless, as the finite creature can never exhaust the resources of the infinite Creator. This was all damaged by the fall, but the picture of the new creation in the Book of Revelation is even more glorious and it remains a dynamic reality because of the potential we will all have to flourish unhindered by the limitations of this present existence. This is especially true when it comes to love and relationships as Paul so beautifully describes in 1 Cor 13. Those who have lived with an intellectual impairment in this life are certainly shaped by that reality and the subsequent lived experience, which in turn has an impact on character and personality. In none of the cases does the healing post-resurrection remove the lived experience, but it does free the person for a new future, in which the potential that was always there becomes actualized for each one of us. We are no longer limited by something that was not essential to our being. Impairment is not a carapace that forever confines the person, but an element of lived experience that provides the framework for dynamic growth in relationships throughout eternity. This love is dynamic, expansive, enabling, enriching, transformative, and freeing.

Living in the Hope

We live in a day and age of contradictions. At one and the same time our culture tends toward terminating the lives of the impaired before birth but after delivery provides more professional support, as well as government and private services than ever before. We live at a time when typically developing people abide by disability discrimination legislation in the public domain but at the same time find it difficult in their private life to include people living with intellectual impairment and their family in a genuine friendship. These contradictions unavoidably call into question the equality and value of people living with intellectual impairment. It is these contradictions that stand at the heart of the two primary concerns of the families we interviewed—an ongoing desire for their son or daughter to be fully recognized and valued as a person, and then to experience deep and abiding friendships. Our interviews revealed that people living with moderate to severe intellectual impairment rarely have friends outside their immediate family and this often results in the social isolation of both the person and their family. This is one of the most damaging realities faced by the family. It is important to acknowledge that many good people provide genuinely helpful support services in both the government and private sectors (both paid and volunteer), but this does not replace the personal friendships that are crucial to the overall well-being of people living with intellectual impairment and their families.

As we have seen, the families and their children almost always prioritize friendship as the critical element that would enable them to cope better with the daily challenges they face. To be a friend to one living with intellectual impairment is to acknowledge their personhood, value and dignity. In Eccl 4:8–12 the writer reflects on the dangers of being "all alone." He says that two people together are better than one who is alone because "If either of them falls down, one can help the other up. But pity anyone who falls and has no one to help them up" (Eccl 12:10). This short passage ends with the statement that while two is good, "A cord of three strands is not quickly broken" (Eccl 12:12). For a Christian, the third strand in the relationship is God, the one for whom *each one matters*, the one who is seeking to be deeply involved in *every person's life,* and the one who reaches out in love to *all* without discrimination. This is the God who, in and through this three-strand cord, invites *every person* to be enveloped within a local community of friends that provide loving, practical support for each other. This is the opportunity that awaits every local church. For it is within the context of practical support being provided by genuine friends that greater hope can emerge for people living with intellectual impairment and their families.

The life and ministry of Jesus demonstrates this unswerving valuing and validation of every single person and the offer of a profoundly deep and enduring friendship to all. This is seen in the two parables we mentioned from Luke 15:1–10 about a lost sheep and a lost coin. The first parable reveals a shepherd who leaves the ninety-nine sheep who are safely gathered to find the one that is lost and vulnerable. The second parable tells of a woman who searches diligently for one lost coin even while she retains nine in her possession. These two parables tell us how important it is to value *each person*, and how important it is to go and seek *each person* who is not currently part of the community, even when it proves to be a costly exercise. This is one of the lessons to be drawn from the parables of "the Good Samaritan" told in Luke 10:25–37 and the "Lost Son" told in Luke 15:11–32. Both parables show us that loving and acting in ways commended by Jesus will be costly in terms of our time, energy, and resources. Beyond highlighting the importance of valuing, seeking, and sacrificing, Jesus, in a very public way, takes the opportunity to remind the religious leaders and teachers of his day that everyone is equally loved by God, including those that they regarded as impaired and therefore had to be isolated from society. He challenges these same communities to genuinely include those they had previously shunned. It is this perspective that lies behind Jesus' very public declaration of the wholeness of the woman who had been physically impaired for twelve years (Luke 8:43–48). This same approach is seen in the accounts of the healing of the woman who had been crippled for eighteen years (Luke 13:10–17), the healing of two men who were blind (Matt 20:29–34), and the restoration of the man thought not to be in his right mind (Mark 5:1–20). In all these situations an encounter with Jesus involved people being called into community. The crippled woman is "brought forward" by Jesus in the synagogue thus indicating his approval of her inclusion in the community; the two blind men who received their sight were "immediately" welcomed into the community of people who "followed him"; and the man from Gerasa is told to "go home to your family." Jesus models how God is forever seeking, forever searching, forever waiting to lavish hospitality on us all. He is forever inviting people to embrace, and be embraced by, community as an essential element of our flourishing.

This is the example we have been called to follow. It begins by seeing that every person is made in the image of God, every person is equally valuable and is to be treated with love and respect. We cannot do this without affirming the vital role of being embraced by a community if we are to truly flourish. Due to the many subtle, and sometimes not so subtle, ways that we are impacted by our Western culture, we may well need to adopt a new perspective on the world and its people. It will be hard to see the face of Christ in our neighbor when we consciously or subconsciously identify them as being a lesser person. It will be hard to have a meaningful friendship with the parents of a child who lives with an intellectual impairment if we do not also extend friendship to their much-loved son or daughter. 1 John 4:19–21 reminds us that "We love because he first loved us. Whoever claims to love God yet hates a brother or sister is a liar. For whoever does not love their brother and sister, whom they have seen, cannot love God, whom they have not seen. And he has given us this command: Anyone who loves God must also love their brother and sister." Empowered by the Holy Spirit, we are called to love with the same quality of love that God in Christ loves us. That quality of love compels us to reform our attitudes and our actions and, for love's sake alone, become agents of change. By intentionally establishing and developing healthy friendships with people who live with intellectual impairment and their families, we will help to arrest the still-evident tendencies toward disengagement and rejection so prevalent in so much of our Western society. The longed-for outcome of our research and reflection is for every Christian, in their small choices and larger decisions, to think and act with a God-given love that demonstrates the heart of Jesus for people whom society so often marginalizes and isolates. Affirmation and friendship begin to bring a longed-for future into the present lived experience of us all. As such, they not only bring hope to the people living with intellectual impairment and their families, but can ultimately change our society for the better, one person, one family at a time.

Bibliography

"About Jesus Club." *Jesus Club*, Dec 18, 2018. Online. https://www.jesusclub.org.au/about.

"Accessible and Inclusive Playgrounds in Brisbane." *Queensland Government*, September 6, 2019. Online. https://www.qld.gov.au/disability/children-young-people/early-childhood/playgrounds.

Albl, Martin. "'For Whenever I Am Weak, Then I Am Strong': Disability in Paul's Epistles." In *Rethinking Disabilities in Biblical Studies,* edited by Hector Avalos et al., 145–58. Atlanta: SBL, 2007.

Albrecht, Gary L., et al., eds. *Handbook of Disability Studies*. Thousand Oaks: Sage, 2001.

Alexander, Denis. "Genes, Determinism and God." *Cambridge Papers* 22.4 (2013) 1–4.

Amundsen, Darrel W. "Medicine and the Birth of Defective Children: Approaches of the Ancient World." In *Euthanasia and the Newborn: Conflicts Regarding Saving Lives*, edited by R. C. McMillan et al., 52–57. Dordrecht: Reidel, 1987.

"Are You Passionate About Social Justice? Do You Want to Support and Empower People with Disabilities in Your Community?" *CBM Australia*, n.d. Online. https://www.cbm.org.au/get-involved/church.

Australian Government, Royal Commission into Institutional Responses to Child Sexual Abuse. "A Brief Guide to the Final Report: Disability." December 15, 2017. Online. https://www.childabuseroyalcommission.gov.au/sites/default/files/a_brief_guide_to_the_final_report_-_disability.pdf.

Australian Human Rights Commission. "Disability Discrimination." November 2014. Online. https://www.humanrights.gov.au/sites/default/files/GPGB_disability_discrimination.pdf.

"Australian Scientist Offers Last Public Thoughts." *Sydney Morning Herald*, May 10, 2018. Online. https://www.smh.com.au/national/australian-scientist-offers-last-public-thoughts-before-swiss-euthanasia-20180510-p4zed8.html.

Baumeister, Roy F., and Mark R. Leary. "The Need to Belong: Desire for Interpersonal Attachments as a Fundamental Human Motivation." *Psychological Bulletin* 117.3 (1995) 497–529.

Berg, Bob. "Give Me Please!" *Journal of Religion, Disability & Health* 13.3 (2009) 181–83.

Bhargava, Dolly. "Personalised Learning Support Plans Used in Education: A Guide for Families." *Developmental Disability Western Australia*, 2017. Online. https://ddwa.org.au/wpcontent/uploads/2017/08/DDWAPersonalisedLearningSupportPlansHandbook-DIGITAL.pdf.

Binger, Nancy. "The 'Options' Parents Need When Their Baby Is Diagnosed with Down Syndrome." *Yahoo Life*, July 17, 2019. Online. https://www.yahoo.com/lifestyle/options-parents-baby-diagnosed-down-191003631.html.

Bird, Michael F. *Evangelical Theology: A Biblical and Systematic Introduction*. Grand Rapids: Zondervan, 2013.

Blevins, Dean G. "The Practicing Self: A Theory of Personhood." *The Asbury Theological Journal* 60.1 (2005) 23–41.

Brower, Francine. "Sensory Issues and Individuals on the Autism Spectrum." Lecture delivered at Nazarene Theological College Brisbane, July 2012.

Brower, Kent. "The Parables of Jesus." Unpublished paper, used with permission.

Brown, Warren S. "Nonreductive Human Uniqueness Immaterial, Biological, or Psychosocial?" In *Human Identity at the Intersection of Science, Technology and Religion*, edited by Nancey Murphey and Christopher C. Knight, 97–115. New York: Routledge, 2016.

———. "Nonreductive Physicalism and the Soul: Finding Resonance Between Theology and Neuroscience." *American Behavioral Scientist* 45.12 (2002) 1812–21.

Browning, Paul. *Principled*. Brisbane: University of Queensland Press, 2020.

Brueggemann, Walter. *The Prophetic Imagination*. Minneapolis: Fortress, 2001.

———. *Texts Under Negotiation: The Bible and Postmodern Imagination*. Minneapolis: Fortress, 1993.

Bryden, Christine. "A Spiritual Journey Into the I-Thou Relationship: A Personal Reflection on Living with Dementia." *Journal of Religion, Spirituality & Aging* 28.1–2 (2016) 7–14.

Bryden, Christine, and Elizabeth MacKinlay. "Dementia—A Spiritual Journey Towards the Divine: A Personal View of Dementia." *Journal of Religious Gerontology* 13.3–4 (2003) 69–75.

Burdett, Michael S. "The Image of God and Human Uniqueness: Challenges from the Biological and Information Sciences." *The Expository Times* 127.1 (2015) 3–10.

Butts, Janie B., and Karen L. Rich. "Acknowledging Dependence: A MacIntyrean Perspective on Relationships Involving Alzheimer's Disease." *Nursing Ethics* 11.4 (2004) 400–410.

Byrne, Brendan. *The Hospitality of God: A Reading of Luke's Gospel*. Collegeville, MD: Liturgical, 2000.

Carse, Alisa L. "Vulnerability, Agency, and Human Flourishing." In *Health and Human Flourishing: Religion, Medicine, and Moral Anthropology*, edited by Carol R. Taylor and Roberto Dell'Oro, 33–52. Washington, DC: Georgetown University Press, 2006.

Carter, Eric W. *Including People with Disabilities in Faith Communities: A Guide for Service Providers, Families, and Congregations*. Baltimore, MD: Paul H. Brookes, 2007.

Castelo, Daniel. *Theological Theodicy*. Eugene, OR: Cascade, 2012.

Centers for Disease Control and Prevention (CDC). "Fragile X Syndrome (FXS)." October 23, 2020. Online. https://www.cdc.gov/ncbddd/fxs.

Collins, Kenneth J. *The Theology of John Wesley: Holy Love and the Shape of Grace*. Nashville: Abingdon, 2007.

"Community Life." *L'Arche Australia*, n.d. Online. https://www.larche.org.au/what-we-do/community-life.

"Community That's Authentic." *Cornerstone Community*, n.d. Online. https://www.cornerstonecommunity.org.au/missional-communities.

Crabbe, Kylie. "A Sinner and a Pharisee: Challenge at Simon's Table in Luke 7:36–50." *Pacifica* 24 (2011) 247–66.

Crispigny, Lachlan J. de, and Julian Savulescu. "Pregnant Women with Fetal Abnormalities: The Forgotten People in the Abortion Debate." *Medical Journal of Australia* 188.2 (2008) 100–103.

Crofford, J. Gregory. *Streams of Mercy: Prevenient Grace in the Theology of John and Charles Wesley*. Lexington: Emeth, 2010.

Daston, Lorraine, and Katharine Park. *Wonders and the Order of Nature, 1150–1750*. New York: Zone, 2001.

Davies, Edward. "Loneliness Is a Modern Scourge, But It Doesn't Have to Be." *Centre for Social Justice*, 2018. Online. http://thecentreforsocialjustice.cmail20.com/t/ViewEmail/y/7CB805AF716F58B3/FC687629C2073D80907C5D7C792C0FF8.

Dawn, Marva J. *Truly the Community: Romans 12 and How to Be the Church*. Grand Rapids: Eerdmans, 1992.

Disability Discrimination Act 1995 (c. 50). Online. https://www.legislation.gov.uk/ukpga/1995/50.

Duggan, Mike. "A Discussion on the Implications of 'Special' Church Services and People Being Treated as Objects of Charity." Unpublished paper, used with permission

———. "Reflections on My Life: Confessions of a Baby Boomer." Unpublished paper, used with permission

———. "A Theology of Disablement: A History of Confusion in the Church Regarding Disability." Unpublished paper, used with permission

Edwards, Martha L. "Constructions of Disability in the Ancient Greek World—The Community Concept." In *The Body and Physical Difference: Discourses of Disability*, edited by David T. Mitchell and Sharon L. Snyder, 35–50. Ann Arbor: University of Michigan Press, 1997.

Eiesland, Nancy L. *The Disabled God: Toward a Liberatory Theology of Disability*. Grand Rapids: Abingdon, 1994.

Eiesland, Nancy L., and Don E. Saliers, eds. *Human Disability and the Service of God*. Grand Rapids: Abingdon, 1998.

Evans, John H. *What Is a Human? What the Answers Mean for Human Rights*. New York: Oxford University Press, 2016.

Flaman, Paul. "Neuroscience, Christian Theology, and a Fuller Understanding of the Human Person." *Religious Education* 106.3 (2011) 252–56.

Franklin, James. "The Lethal Philosophy of Peter Singer." *Quadrant*, August 23, 2012. Online. https://quadrant.org.au/magazine/2012/09/the-lethal-philosophy-of-peter-singer.

Gale, Lindsay. "Christian Ministry to People Affected by Disability—Summer 08/09." *EFAC*, February 13, 2009. Online. https://www.efac.org.au/index.php/2009/summer-20089/christian-ministry-affected-by-disability.

Garland-Thomson, Rosemarie. "Conserving Disability and Constructing a Habitable World." *Australian Broadcasting Corporation*, December 3, 2020. Online. https://www.abc.net.au/religion/rosemarie-garland-thomson-conserving-disability-and-constructin/12408108.

Goodall, Margaret. "Caring for People with Dementia: A Sign of the Kingdom." *International Journal of Practical Theology* 18.2 (2014) 253–54.

Green, Joel B. "The Gospel of Luke." In *International Commentary on the New Testament*, edited by Ned B. Stonehouse et al., 342–49. Grand Rapids: Eerdmans, 1997.

Grenz, Stanley. *The Social God and the Relational Self: A Trinitarian Theology of the Imago Dei*. Louisville: Westminster John Knox, 1998.

Hagner, Donald A. *Matthew 14–28*. Word Biblical Commentary 33b. Dallas: Word, 1995.

Hamel, Ronald P. "Health Policy and a Theological Anthropology." In *Health and Human Flourishing*, edited by Carol R. Taylor and Roberto Dell'Oro, 231–40. Washington, DC: Georgetown University Press, 2006.

———. *The Roman Catholic Tradition: Religious Beliefs and Healthcare Decisions*. Updated by Kevin O'Rourke. Religious Traditions and Healthcare Decisions. Park Ridge, IL: Park Ridge Center for the Study of Health, Faith, and Ethics, 2002.

Harrison, Peter. *The Bible, Protestantism and the Rise of Natural Science*. Cambridge: Cambridge University Press, 1998.

Hauerwas, Stanley. "The Church and the Mentally Handicapped." *Journal of Religion, Disability & Health* 8.3 (2005) 53–62.

———. "Timeful Friends." *Journal of Religion, Disability & Health* 8.3 (2005) 11–25.

Hedges-Goettl, Barbara J. "Thinking Theologically About Inclusion." *Journal of Religion Disability & Health* 6.4 (2002) 7–30.

Hefner, Philip. "Imago Dei: The Possibility and Necessity of the Human Person." In *Questioning the Human: Toward a Theological Anthropology for the Twenty-First Century*, edited by Lieven Boeve et al., 73–94. New York: Fordham University Press, 2014.

Hely, Jack. "Hospitality as a Sign and Sacrament." *Journal of Religion, Disability & Health* 6.4 (2002) 67–80.

Herzfeld, Noreen LuAnn. "*Imago Dei/Imago Hominis*: Interacting Images of God and Humanity in Theology and in Artificial Intelligence." PhD diss., Graduate Theological Union, Berkeley, CA, 1999.

Hewlett, Martinez. "What Does It Mean to Be Human? Genetics and Human Identity." In *Issues in Science and Theology: Are We Special? Human Uniqueness in Science and Theology*, edited by Michael Fuller et al., 147–63. Issues in Science and Religion: Publications of the European Society for the Study of Science and Theology 4. Cham, Switzerland: Springer, 2017.

Heyes, Cecilia. "Cognitive Gadgets." *Aeon*, April 17, 2019. Online. https://aeon.co/essays/how-culture-works-with-evolution-to-produce-human-cognition.

Hicks, Peter. "One or Two? A Historical Survey of an Aspect of Personhood." *Evangelical Quarterly* 77.1 (2005) 35–45.

Hingsburger, Dave. "First Communion." *Journal of Religion, Disability & Health* 13.3 (2009) 173–74.

Hogue, David. "Brain Matters: Neuroscience, Empathy, and Pastoral Theology." *Journal of Pastoral Theology* 20.2 (2010) 25–55.

Holt-Lunstad, Julia, et al., "Advancing Social Connection as a Public Health Priority in the United States." *American Psychologist* 72.6 (2017) 517–30.

Hudson, Rosalie E. "Dementia and Personhood: A Living Death or Alive in God?" *Colloquium* 36.2 (2004) 123–42.

———. "God's Faithfulness and Dementia: Christian Theology in Context." *Journal of Religion, Spirituality & Aging* 28.1–2 (2016) 50–67.

Hughes, Melanie D. "The Holistic Way: John Wesley's Practical Piety as a Resource for Integrated Healthcare." *Journal of Religion and Health* 47.2 (2008) 237–52.

Hull, John M. "The Broken Body in a Broken World." *Journal of Religion Disability & Health* 7.4 (2004) 5–23.

BIBLIOGRAPHY

Human Rights Commission, New Zealand [Te Kāhui Tika Tangata] (HRCNZ). "Disability Rights." n.d. Online. https://www.hrc.co.nz/your-rights/your-rights.

Hurley, Kate. *Take Heart: For Families Living with Disability*. Sydney: Blue Bottle, 2008.

"Joni & Friends: Sharing Hope through Hardship." *Joni & Friends*, n.d. Online. https://www.joniandfriends.org.

Judge, Stuart J. "Nothing but a Pack of Neurons?" *Faraday Paper* 16 (2010) 1–4.

Julian of Norwich. *Revelations of Divine Love*. Translated by Grace Warrack. London: Methuen & Co., 1901. Online. https://ccel.org/ccel/julian/revelations/revelations.i.html.

Keck, Leander E. *Luke—John*. The New Interpreter's Bible 9. Nashville: Abingdon, 1996.

Kelly, Nicole. "Deformity and Disability in Greece and Rome." In *Rethinking Disabilities in Biblical Studies*, edited by Hector Avalos et al., 31–46. Atlanta: SBL, 2007.

Kinghorn, Warren A. "'I Am Still with You': Dementia and the Christian Wayfarer." *Journal of Religion, Spirituality & Aging* 28.1–2 (2016) 98–117.

Kleinig, John, and Nicholas G. Evans. "Human Flourishing, Human Dignity, and Human Rights." *Law and Philosophy* 32.5 (2013) 539–64.

Knight, Henry H., III. *The Presence of God in the Christian Life: John Wesley and the Means of Grace*. Lanham: Scarecrow, 1992.

Kyriacou, Jen. "How to Talk to My Child with a Disability and How to Include Her." *SourceKids* (blog), n.d. Online. https://www.sourcekids.com.au/how-to-talk-to-my-child-with-a-disability.

"The L'Arche Story in Australia." *L'Arche Australia*, n.d. Online. https://www.larche.org.au/about-us/the-larche-story-in-australia.

Lawnton, Robert B. "Genesis 2:24: Trite or Tragic?" *Journal of Biblical Literature* 105.1 (1986) 97–98.

Lewis, C. S. *The Weight of Glory*. New ed. San Francisco: HarperOne, 2001.

Lumbreras, Sara. "Strong Artificial Intelligence and *Imago Hominis*: The Risks of a Reductionist Definition of Human Nature." In *Issues in Science and Theology: Are We Special? Human Uniqueness in Science and Theology*, edited by Michael Fuller et al., 157–68. Issues in Science and Religion: Publications of the European Society for the Study of Science and Theology 4. Cham, Switzerland: Springer, 2017.

Luo, Liquin. "Why Is the Human Brain So Efficient? How Massive Parallelism Lifts the Brain's Performance Above That of AI." *Nautilus* 59 (2018). Online. http://nautil.us/issue/59/connections/why-is-the-human-brain-so-efficient.

Madden, Deborah. *A "Cheap, Safe and Natural Medicine": Religion, Medicine and Culture in John Wesley's "Primitive Physic."* Leiden: Brill, 2007.

Maddox, Randy L. "John Wesley—Practical Theologian?" *Wesleyan Theological Journal* 23 (1988) 122–47.

———. *Responsible Grace: John Wesley's Practical Theology*. Nashville: Kingswood, 1994.

McEwan, David B. *The Life of God in the Soul: The Integration of Love, Holiness and Happiness in the Thought of John Wesley*. Milton Keynes: Paternoster, 2015.

———. "Personal and Community Well-Being: A Wesleyan Theological Framework for Overcoming Prejudice." In *Wellbeing, Personal Wholeness and the Social Fabric: An Interdisciplinary Approach*, edited by Doru Costache et al., 132–53. Newcastle: Cambridge Scholars, 2017.

———. "Whose Body, Whose Life, Whose Decision? A Wesleyan Reflection on Personal Autonomy, Interdependence, and Human Flourishing." *Wesley and Methodist Studies* 12.1 (2020) 47–70.

McFarlane, Graham. "Living on the Edge—Moving Towards the Centre: The Place of Jesus Christ in Our Quest for Personhood." *Evangelical Quarterly* 78.1 (2006) 37–50.

McGilchrist, Iain. *The Master and His Emissary: The Divided Brain and the Making of the Western World*. 2nd ed. New Haven: Yale University Press, 2019.

McGrath, Alister E. "The Ideological Uses of Evolutionary Biology in Recent Atheist Apologetics." In *Biology and Ideology from Descartes to Dawkins*, edited by Denis R. Alexander and Ronald L. Numbers, 329–51. Chicago: University of Chicago Press, 2010.

McReady, Wayne O., and Adele Reinhartz, *Common Judaism: Explorations in Second-Temple Judaism*. Minneapolis: Fortress, 2008.

Midgley, Mary. "Consciousness, Fatalism and Science." In *Questioning the Human: Toward a Theological Anthropology for the Twenty-First Century*, edited by Lieven Boeve et al., 21–40. New York: Fordham University Press, 2014.

Mitchelson, Alana. "Down Syndrome Abortions Increasing as Parents React to Testing." *New Daily*, August 17, 2017. Online. https://thenewdaily.com.au/news/national/2017/08/17/down-syndrome-birth-terminations.

Moltmann, Jurgen. "Liberate Yourselves by Accepting One Another." In *Human Disability and the Service of God*, edited by Nancy L. Eiesland and Don E. Saliers, 105–22. Nashville: Abingdon, 1998.

Morris, Wayne. "Church as Sign and Alternative: Disabled People in the Churches." *Journal of Religion, Disability & Health* 14.1 (2010) 47–59.

Motyer, Steve. "'Not Apart from Us' (Hebrews 11:40): Physical Community in the Letter to the Hebrews." *Evangelical Quarterly* 77.3 (2005) 235–47.

National Disability Insurance Scheme (NDIS). "Understanding the National Disability Insurance Scheme." n.d. Online. https://www.ndis.gov.au.

Nielsen, Lilli. *Are You Blind?* Copenhagen: Sikon, 2003.

———. *The FIELA Curriculum: 730 Learning Environments*. Copenhagen: Sikon, 1998.

Noble, Thomas A. "East and West in the Theology of John Wesley." *Bulletin of the John Rylands Library* 85.2 (2003) 359–72.

———. *Holy Trinity, Holy People: The Theology of Christian Perfecting*. Eugene, OR: Cascade, 2013.

Nolland, John. *Luke 1–9:20*. Word Biblical Commentary 35a. Dallas: Word, 1989.

Nouwen, Henri. *Adam: God's Beloved*. Blackburn, Victoria: Harper Collins Religious, 1997.

O'Clery, Cian, dir. *Employable Me*. 2 seasons, 6 episodes. ABC Australia. April 3, 2018–April 23, 2019.

Olyan, Saul M. "Anyone Blind or Lame Shall Not Enter the House: On the Interpretation of Second Samuel 5:8b." *The Catholic Biblical Quarterly* 60.2 (1998) 218–27.

———. *Disability in the Hebrew Bible: Interpreting Mental and Physical Differences*. New York: Cambridge University Press, 2008.

———. "The Exegetical Dimensions of Restrictions on the Blind and the Lame in Texts from Qumran." *Dead Sea Discoveries* 8 (2001) 38–50.

Peckham, Colin N. *John Wesley's Understanding of Human Infirmities*. Ilkeston: Wesley Fellowship, 1997.

Phelps, Stephen H. "Luke 13:10–17." *Interpretation* 55.1 (2001) 64–66.

Polanyi, Michael. *Personal Knowledge: Towards a Post-Critical Philosophy*. London: Routledge and Kegan Paul, 1958.

———. *Science, Faith and Society*. Chicago: University of Chicago Press, 1964.

Porter, Roy. *The Creation of the Modern World: The Untold Story of the British Enlightenment*. New York: Norton, 2000.

Pridmore, Eric. "The Christian Reformed Church as a Model for the Inclusion of People with Disabilities." *Journal of Religion, Disability & Health* 10.1 (2006) 93–107.

Rack, Henry D. *Reasonable Enthusiast: John Wesley and the Rise of Methodism*. London: Epworth: 2002.

Reinders, Hans S. *Receiving the Gift of Friendship: Profound Disability, Theological Anthropology, and Ethics*. Grand Rapids: Eerdmans, 2008.

Reist, Melinda Tankard. *Defiant Birth: Women Who Resist Medical Eugenics*. North Melbourne: Spinifex, 2006.

Reynolds, Thomas E. *Vulnerable Communion: A Theology of Disability and Hospitality*. Grand Rapids: Brazos, 2008.

Right to Life New South Wales (NSW). "Abortion." *Right to Life NSW*, April 29, 2020. Online. https://righttolifensw.org.au/be-informed/abortion.

Roberts-Mazzeo, Natalie. "The Hidden Workload of a Special Needs Parent." *SourceKids* (blog), August 8, 2017. Online. https://www.sourcekids.com.au/the-hidden-workload-of-a-special-needs-parent.

Rogers, Charles A. "The Concept of Prevenient Grace in the Theology of John Wesley." PhD diss., Duke University, 1967.

Romensky, Larissa. "Down Syndrome: Crossroad That Leads to Choices for Parents of an Unborn Child with the Condition." *Australian Broadcasting Corporation*, July 16, 2017. Online. https://mobile.abc.net.au/news/2017-07-17/the-choices-for-parents-of-an-unborn-child-with-down-syndrome/8708836.

Roozeboom, William D. *Neuroplasticity, Performativity, and Clergy Wellness: Neighbor Love as Self-Care*. Lanham: Lexington, 2017.

———. "Rethinking Theological Anthropology: Constructing a Pastoral Theology of Wellness in Light of the Paradigm of Plasticity in Neuroscience." PhD diss., Brite Divinity School, 2013.

Rosner, Brian S. *Known by God: A Biblical Theology of Personal Identity*. Grand Rapids: Zondervan, 2017.

Samuelson, Calum. *Artificially Intelligent? Grappling with the Myths, Present Realities, and Future Trajectories of AI*. Cambridge: Jubilee Centre, 2019.

Sheriffs, Deryck. "'Personhood' in the Old Testament? Who's Asking?" *Evangelical Quarterly* 77.1 (2005) 13–34.

Short, Monica. *Anglican Churches Engaging with People Living with Disabilities*. Sydney: Bush Aid Society of Australia, 2018.

Singer, Peter. *Practical Ethics*. 2nd ed. New York: Cambridge University Press, 1993.

———. *Rethinking Life & Death*. New York: St Martin's; Griffin, 1996.

Solomon, Andrew. *Far from the Tree*. New York: Scribner, 2012.

Spicer, William, and James Moore, dirs. *Mission to Lars*. Written by James Moore. London: Mission Films, 2012.

Starling, David. "The Very Practical Doctrine of Total Depravity." *The Briefing* 363 (2008) 10–13.

Stiker, Henri-Jacques. *A History of Disability*. Translated by William Sayers. Ann Arbor: University of Michigan Press, 1999.

Stone, Selina. "Resisting the Powers That Oppress." *London Institute for Contemporary Christianity*, July 6, 2020. Online. https://www.licc.org.uk/resources/resisting-the-powers.

Swinton, John. *Building a Church for Strangers*. Edinburgh: Contact Pastoral Trust, 1999.

———. "Introduction: Hauerwas on Disability." *Journal of Religion, Disability & Health* 8.3 (2005) 1–9.

———. "Known by God." In *The Paradox of Disability: Responses to Jean Vanier and L'Arche Communities from Theology and the Sciences*, edited by Hans S. Reinders, 140–53. Grand Rapids: Eerdmans, 2010.

———. *Raging with Compassion: Pastoral Responses to the Problem of Evil*. Grand Rapids: Eerdmans, 2007.

Taylor, Carol. "Health Care and a Theological Anthropology." In *Health and Human Flourishing*, edited by Carol R. Taylor and Roberto Dell'Oro, 225–29. Washington, DC: Georgetown University Press, 2006.

Thompson, Jon. "Christianity: The True Humanism." *Cambridge Papers* 21.4 (2012) 1–4.

Torrance, James. "The Doctrine of the Trinity in Our Contemporary Situation." In *The Forgotten Trinity: A Selection of Papers Presented to the BCC Study Commission on Trinitarian Doctrine Today*, edited by Alisdair I. C. Herron, 3–17. London: BCC/CCBI Inter-Church House, 1991.

Turner, Max. "Approaching 'Personhood' in the New Testament, with Special Reference to Ephesians." *Evangelical Quarterly* 77.3 (2005) 212–13.

United Nations (UN) General Assembly. *Convention on the Rights of the Child*. Resolution 44/25, November 20, 1989. Online. https://www.ohchr.org/documents/professionalinterest/crc.pdf.

———. *Universal Declaration of Human Rights*. 217 (III) A, December 10, 1948. Online. http://www.un.org/en/universal-declaration-human-rights.

VanderPlaats, Dan. "Maybe It's All in the Attitude: Every Christian Is on a Journey of Disability Attitudes." *All Belong Center for Inclusive Education* (blog), n.d. Online. https://allbelong.org/maybe-its-all-in-the-attitude.

Wassen, Cecilia. "What Do Angels Have Against the Blind and the Deaf? Rules of Exclusion in the Dead Sea Scrolls." In *Common Judaism: Explorations in Second Temple Judaism*, edited by Wayne O. McRdeady and Adele Reinhartz, 115–30. Minneapolis: Fortress, 2008.

Watt, Amanda. "Amy Illidge, Doctor, 38, Woolloongabba." *QWeekend*, May 23, 2020. 4.

Watts, Fraser. "The Multifaceted Nature of Human Personhood: Psychological and Theological Perspectives." In *Questioning the Human: Toward a Theological Anthropology for the Twenty-First Century*, edited by Lieven Boeve et al., 41–63. New York: Fordham University Press, 2014.

Wax, Trevin. "Being Attentive to Your Attention." *The Gospel Coalition* (blog), May 19, 2020. Online. https://www.thegospelcoalition.org/blogs/trevin-wax/being-attentive-to-your-attention.

Webb-Mitchell, Brett. "Confession: A Journey Toward Reconciliation between the Church and People with Disabilities." *Liturgy* 23.2 (2008) 47–55.

Wesley, John. *Doctrinal and Controversial Treatises II*. Edited by Paul Wesley Chilcote and Kenneth J. Collins. Vol. 13 of *The Works of John Wesley*. Nashville: Abingdon, 2013.

———. *Journals and Diaries V (1765–1775)*. Edited by W. Reginald Ward and Richard P. Heitzenrater. Vol. 22 of *The Works of John Wesley*. Nashville: Abingdon, 1993.

———. *Journals and Diaries VI (1766–1786)*. Edited by W. Reginald Ward and Richard P. Heitzenrater. Vol. 23 of *The Works of John Wesley*. Nashville: Abingdon, 1995.

———. *Letters I (1729–1739)*. Edited by Frank Baker. Vol. 25 of *The Works of John Wesley*. Oxford ed. Nashville: Abingdon, 1980.

———. *The Letters of the Rev. John Wesley.* Edited by John Telford. Vols. 1–8. London: Epworth, 1931.

———. *Medical and Health Writings.* Edited by James G. Donat and Randy L. Maddox. Vol. 32 of *The Works of John Wesley.* Nashville: Abingdon, 2018.

———. *The Methodist Societies: History, Nature, and Design.* Edited by Rupert E. Davies. Vol. 9 of *The Works of John Wesley.* Nashville: Abingdon, 1989.

———. *The Methodist Societies: The Minutes of the Conference.* Edited by Henry D. Rack. Vol. 10 of *The Works of John Wesley.* Nashville: Abingdon, 2011.

———. *Sermons.* Edited by Albert C. Outler. Vols. 1–4. Nashville: Abingdon, 1984–1987.

Westermann, Claus. *Genesis 1–11: A Commentary.* London: SPCK, 1984.

"What is the Americans with Disabilities Act (ADA)?" *ADA National Network*, n.d. Online. https://adata.org/learn-about-ada.

Wheatley, Edward. *Stumbling Blocks Before the Blind: Medieval Constructions of a Disability.* Ann Arbor: University of Michigan Press, 2010.

Whitney, Trevor. "Intellectual Disability and Holy Communion: The Peace that Passes Understanding." *Journal of Religion, Disability & Health* 13.3 (2009) 247–59.

Wilson, Michael P. "Theological Reflections on Entering the World of the Disabled—The First Tremors of an Earthquake?" *Epworth Review* 31.4 (2004) 16–24.

Wyatt, John. "Quality of Life." *Christian Medical Fellowship Files* 30 (2005) 1–4.

Yong, Amos. *Theology and Down Syndrome: Reimagining Disability in Late Modernity.* Waco: Baylor University Press, 2007.

Young, Frances. *God's Presence: A Contemporary Recapitulation of Early Christianity.* New York: Cambridge University Press, 2013.

Zizioulas, John D. *Being as Communion: Studies in Personhood and the Church.* Crestwood: St. Vladimir's Seminary Press, 2000.

———. "On Being a Person: Towards an Ontology of Personhood." In *Persons, Divine and Human*, edited by Christopher Schwobel and Colin E. Gunton, 99–112. Edinburgh: T&T Clark, 1991.

www.ingramcontent.com/pod-product-compliance
Lightning Source LLC
Chambersburg PA
CBHW071502150426
43191CB00009B/1404